Jan

M

J

OTHERWORLDLINESS AND THE NEW TESTAMENT

AMOS N. WILDER

OTHERWORLDLINESS

AND THE NEW TESTAMENT

HARPER & BROTHERS

PUBLISHERS, NEW YORK

Library of Congress catalogue card number: 54–11661

FOREWORD

The incentive to the writing of the present volume
was afforded by invitations to lecture on two similar
foundations: that of the Jackson Lectureship at the
Perkins School of Theology and that of the John C.
Shaffer Lectureship at the Yale Divinity School. In
the lectures at Dallas in February, 1954, the first and
the last two of the chapters that follow were presented
(together with a lecture not here included) under the
topic: "Commending the Gospel in Our Time." I wish
to record here my appreciation of the many kind-
nesses shown me during my visit by Dean Merrimon
Cuniggim and the Faculty of the Perkins School of
Theology, and again to make my acknowledgment to
Mrs. Lizzie Jackson Davenport and Mr. Mims J.
Jackson, representing the donors, who were present.
The Shaffer Lectures, comprising the four chapters
that follow, were given at the Yale Divinity School in
April, 1954. I take this occasion to express my warm
thanks to Dean Liston Pope and the Faculty of the
School for their generous hospitality in connection
with the Convocation and the Lectures.

The one great and telling charge made against the
Christian religion in the modern period is that it is
otherworldly, escapist and irrelevant to the problems
of this life. With this accusation can be associated the
names of Karl Marx, Nietzsche and Sir James Frazer,
but it recurs in many forms among modern writers
and conditions the attitudes of multitudes. It must be
admitted that many expressions of Christianity are
vulnerable at this point. Even where they do not lay
excessive stress on the world to come, they are falsely
spiritualistic, or they identify the Gospel with noble
but ineffectual ideas and ideals, or they confine the
life of the faithful to private exercises whether refined or orgiastic.

It is true that our antagonists and critics are often
ill-qualified to pass judgment on the faith. They may
be amiable Philistines who confuse the simple order
of enjoyments of which they are capable with the
proper depth and altitude of human experience. They
may be modern Graeculi or diminished heirs of a
classical tradition who still identify Hebraism with
barbarism, or cultists of a pagan vitality who similarly shrink when the Scripture speaks of "justice,
and self-control and future judgment." They may
count themselves among the emancipated who repu-
diate as "fictions" most of what the world has es-
teemed precious, whether it has come from Palestine
or Greece, from East or West. They may be converts

to Marxism or to scientific humanism who in place of the otherworldly faith which they scorn as "compensatory" accept a this-worldly mythology and Utopianism far more naïve.

Yet even when we make allowance for all such erroneous views, we must take seriously the widespread indictment made against the church and the faith. Christians themselves have a bad conscience in this matter. The everrecurrent plea of the layman today that religion should be made relevant to his problems is an index of the situation.

The present volume seeks to come to terms with this issue. The crux of the whole matter lies in the New Testament itself. Heretical forms of otherworldliness have appeared in the church through all the centuries and have always appealed to the Scriptures. Contemporary forms of escapism and false spirituality rest upon a misunderstanding of the Gospels and the other writings of the New Testament. There is no question but that the evangelists and the apostles used pictorial otherworldly categories, interpreted the crisis in which they lived in dualistic terms, and directed their attention toward an imminent consummation of the divine plan. The circumstances of the earliest believers inevitably conditioned their outlook and help to account for certain features of asceticism in their attitudes. Yet we can easily misunderstand the New Testament and the whole character of Christianity if we do not look behind these early formulations.

The Christian faith has its transcendent dimensions. In what follows I do not propose to minimize these. It is natural that theologians should recognize these transcendent realities by drawing sharp distinctions between the human and the divine, between the temporal and the eternal. This procedure has every justification. We should not, however, divorce these genuinely otherworldly realities from our common human experience. Only as they are kept together can the valid otherworldliness of the Gospel remain sound and healthy. With reference to the historical origins of Christianity this means that we should not slight the social and cultural factors through which revelation was mediated and to which it spoke. If this sounds like a truism I would only observe that its full significance is often missed. The all importance of the divine initiative and the formal dichotomies of the New Testament lead us to obscure the way in which God's work is related to what we may call the secular and natural factors in human experience.

The fact that the men of the Bible represent the operations of God as sudden and unaccountable, his choice of his agents as a matter of the divine counsel hidden to human standards, his revelations as unrelated to second causes: all this represents an understandable acknowledgment of the disparity between creator and creature, between the eternal and the temporal. Modern faith, voicing itself in worship and devotion, inevitably recurs to the same antitheses. But we may surely also take account of the fact that the men of the Bible had their own categories for interpreting causation and historical forces, categories which are far removed from the terms of our modern quest for understanding.

The fact that the men of the Bible, in witnessing to their right sense of the majesty of God, employ symbols which dramatize the contrasts between flesh and spirit, between earthly and heavenly agency, has every justification. It is by such mythopoetic images alone that such great themes can be adequately reported, and they have the added advantage of their social character and long cumulative associations. But they should not mislead us into adopting a systematic dualism or theology of discontinuity. The pictorial vehicles should be read as such, and not translated into prose nor displaced from their original setting without great circumspection.

The fact that the men of the New Testament set forth the destiny of man and the world in dualistic terms and portray the goals of providence in sublime and otherworldly colors: this we may be grateful for as their witness to the supreme intimations of faith. But we do ill to carry over their language in a literal way or to exclude all such auguries from any application to the future of men in this world.

In my own thought I note a double influence at work in the following chapters. On the one hand I recognize an empirical tradition in our American way of looking at things which invites us constantly to scrutinize any tendency to an unreal dualism or separation of faith from life. I also feel myself indebted to those who have explored the social conditioning of the religious life. In this connection I record a special debt to a long tradition at the University of Chicago, and take this occasion to acknowledge my gratitude to my colleagues during these past years in the Chicago Theological Seminary and in the Federated Theological Faculty of the University.

Chicago   Amos N. Wilder
May, 1954

OTHERWORLDLINESS AND THE NEW TESTAMENT

1

MODERN FAITH AND THE CHARGE OF OTHERWORLDLINESS

I   We live in a time when the ancient Bible and its faith are subject to radical misunderstanding. They are offered to men in extraordinarily diverse ways. A glance at the church announcements of a metropolitan newspaper or the turning of the dial of the radio on Sunday morning will bring this home to us. What a charivari, what a confusion, what a disheartening anarchy of views one meets today whether within the churches or without. Every man one meets and every sect one encounters have their special conceptions or misconceptions, their stray fragment of life-giving insight, but also their curious distortion if not travesty of the truth. And what diverse fictions are current in the public as to biblical history! "Is it possible," wrote the poet Rilke in another connection, "that all these people have such a perfect knowledge of a past that never existed!" [1] Indeed, all makes for contradiction, exasperation and weakness.

---

[1] *"Est-il possible que tous ces gens connaissent parfaitement un passé qui n'a jamais existé?"* Les cahiers de Malte Laurids Brigge (Paris, 1926), p. 30.

It is not surprising that many are led by this situation to religious indifference if not hostility. In any case the movement of the times has alienated large groups from the churches, conservative or liberal. Many men do not find their needs met and they do not find themselves spoken to by the message of the pulpit or the altar. The words of Scripture have an archaic or unreal ring about them to the layman, to youth, to those in the armed forces. Even where the Bible, and the words and figure of the Christ, exert their inherent power upon the conscience of the disaffected, active membership in the Christian church is blocked by many factors. And believers *within* the churches will too often confess that they must take, as they say, "on faith," those deeper realities to which their ministers appeal—such as the meaning of the life "in Christ" or the indispensable role of personal prayer or the inner significance of the Lord's Supper.

Thus the Christian faith takes on a character of unreality. It is this situation which has occasioned the various radical efforts today to revitalize and modernize the Scripture and its message: such as that of neo-orthodoxy to lift up the single august theme of the Word of God in Christ as a voice speaking directly to the soul of man apart from all distractions of human culture or church traditions; or that of scholars like C. H. Dodd to find the center of the New Testament message; or of the World Council of Churches through its Study Department to define biblical authority for the great social and political problems of our time; or efforts like that of Rudolf Bultmann to reinterpret the alien conceptions and old-world pictures in which the Gospel is addressed to men in the New Testament.

For our dilemma is more than one of sectarianism or of religious illiteracy. We live today in a great revolutionary epoch. The Gospel has to transplant itself into a new world that is emerging at the same time that it continues its witness where the older landscape remains. The situation is like that faced by Paul and his fellow missioners who went out into the Gentile world. Today the church has a new mission field right here all about us. A new kind of man has appeared as a result of modern experience in our age of technology and world wars. This new type is shaped by different forces, and many old and familiar patterns, bonds and sentiments are lost and dissolved for him. He speaks a different language. It is astonishing how rapidly this new breed multiplies. It captures the ranks of youth and the student bodies of our colleges and universities to the bewilderment of the older instructors. When we speak to these new men we find that we are speaking to strangers. They do not live where we live!

But there are some very good things that can be

said about this new kind of man. He is a modern. He is free from many of the limitations of his fathers and forefathers. While he is alienated from many of the patterns of the past he is not virulently hostile. He wants to be shown. He is in fact in distress, in anxiety. He has no ground under his feet. He offers a good field for the Christian message.

Paul and his contemporaries carried the Gospel of the Jewish Messiah across a bridge over to a Gentile world of strangers, many of whom did not know what the word "Messiah" (i.e. "Christ") meant. We in our day have just as great a bridge to cross if we would have our faith make sense to the modern man.

There is one problem which is crucial today for the church and its message. It is the problem of this-worldliness and otherworldliness. It has many aspects. We all realize that the Scriptures and the Christian faith have their crowning glory in that they relate us to God, admit us to the life eternal even here, and answer questions that have to do with Alpha and Omega. If to believe these things is to be otherworldly and escapist, we plead guilty.

But we also know that the Gospel has taken on many distorted forms of otherworldliness. We can well generalize and say that the one great and telling accusation made against the Christian religion in our modern period is that it is "escapist," that it evades

responsibility for the problems of our life in this
world. Here indeed our faith is really vulnerable.[2]
The strength of the attack of Marxism upon the Gospel lies here. Nietzsche is only one of a long line of
influential modern prophets and writers who have re-
proached Christianity for its false spirituality or false
asceticism. The indifference or disaffection of multitudes of men today, secularists or freethinkers or ag-
nostics, whatever they call themselves, is part of the
same picture. Their way of putting it is to say that the
Gospel as it is offered is unreal or irrelevant.

Thus many of our contemporaries are inclined to
say that the Christian conviction of things not seen
and the Resurrection hope mean escapism, pie-in-the-
sky, the opium of the people, what they call "compensatory fictions." [3] How hard it is to prove to such

[2] Cf. N. Berdyaev, "Grounds for Hostility to Christianity," *The
Student World*, XXXI, 1938, pp. 106–14. The special emphasis of the
author here is on the charge that Christianity demeans man, views
him as impotent, and thus reconciles him to acceptance of his lot,
sealing this slave mentality by offering otherworldly consolations
and promises. See also the article by Paul Tillich which follows the
above: "The Attack of Dialectical Materialism on Christianity," pp.
115–25.

[3] The man in the street is shrewdly aware of these deformations in
much Christianity as taught and practiced. One could make a list of
the often merciless jibes that are current, phrases which betray at
once the Philistine in him and the faults of some Christians. Whatever the failing he has a word for it: plaster-of-Paris saints, Holy
Joes, swooning mystics, cataleptic revivalists, jaundiced Sabbatarians,
professional do-gooders, weeping Jeremiahs, anemic Galahads, religious masochists, etc.

skeptics that there is no contradiction between genuine otherworldliness and the life abundant here and now, between the heavenly manna and daily bread. There must be something wrong about the way Christians live for these great libels on the Gospel to win such a hold! And what specially interests us here, there must be something wrong about the way we interpret the New Testament.

We know that these groups and individuals misunderstand the faith. Yet the modern church has often given them grounds for the error. In various ways we have separated faith from life and made that faith unreal.

II   Now let us take a closer look at this great handicap which the churches suffer today in trying to cross the bridge of which we have spoken. The characteristic heresy of modern Christianity, whether liberal or orthodox or neo-orthodox, is the false spirituality of its message and life. We are not specially concerned at this point with overemphasis on the afterlife. We are more concerned with our various kinds of escapism or irrelevance as regards this life. Justice should of course be done to the practical and humanitarian bent of much of our activity. This is good and it is one of the redeeming features of our American Protestantism.

Nevertheless, we are afflicted with a kind of dualism which locates Christian experience in the soul rather than in the whole man, in the feelings rather than in the will. Even when we recognize that religion is a matter of the heart we do not use the word "heart" as it is used in the Bible, where it means our whole natural make-up, reason, feeling and will, in our relation to God and our fellows.[4]

Our understanding of religion tends to short-cut a great deal of our human nature, and we are only partly baptized. We connect God with our religious ideals, sentiments and feelings, and overlook the importance for him of those deep dynamic impulses, drives, instincts which come into play in our everyday secular lives. But this means that our Christian life loses power. Its taproots are cut. We forget that grace and revelation come to men not through their heads and hearts, but through the elemental factors in their human nature, through the commonplace but fateful aspects of our mortality, such as family relationships, patriotism, making a living, growing old.

[4] Note the remarks of the French scholar Théo Preiss with reference to Paul's words: "The love of God is shed abroad in our hearts." Preiss writes: "It is necessary to underline in large characters that the word 'heart' does not mean, as it is almost always understood, a capacity, a faculty, an aspect of our being by which we should be nearer to God than by reason. In the Bible the 'heart' designates the intimate center and the totality of the human personality where intelligence, feeling, and will reside." *Interpretation*, VII, 3, July, 1953, p. 274.

It is in such areas that God works and reveals himself, blesses and judges. This is what incarnation means. The Bible is almost dismayingly human in this sense. Its great message and hope rest upon a prior operation of salvage carried out at cost at this elemental level. We tend to think that Christianity began as a matter of ideas and ideals rather than as a bloody drama involving men's primordial relationships and loyalties and as a succession of trials, imprisonments, excommunications and family cleavages. We think of Jesus as an inspired teacher and example or as a theological God-man, and forget that he was also a patriot, and that there is a connection between the two. We think of Paul also in a kind of abstraction if we forget that his calling came to him through his very human agonized reappraisal of the way of his fathers.

This tendency toward otherworldiness in Christianity has, of course, a long history. In ancient Israel there was no cleavage between body and soul, nor between man and nature. The soul could not be redeemed without the body, and man could not be redeemed by taking him out of nature. But the Greek world had become increasingly conscious of the gulf between nature and spirit. The tension between the two led in the Hellenistic period to a craving for release *from* nature and *from* the flesh, by all manner of religious disciplines, by meditation, asceticism and sacrament. This outlook impressed itself upon early

Christianity in various forms, good and bad, and tended to obscure the biblical wholeness and realism.

In the modern period a dualistic development has its corresponding historical causes. We are the heirs of a long period in which all aspects of the spiritual and also the esthetic life have been shunted off onto a sidetrack; assigned to a special compartment; banished from the market place and the crude realities of life; put upon a pedestal or relegated to a shrine. In part it began with the rising sway of science and the false distinctions made between intellect and values. In another aspect it developed with the age of sentiment and the Romantic movement which encouraged both the believer and the artist in an intense spirituality over against the world of practical things and later over against the Leviathan of modern economic and social power. Religious and artistic experience were led to make a home for themselves in the soul, in the emotions and the imagination, and to surrender their claim upon the whole of life. They settled for the eternal and thought they had a good bargain. But the temporal and the historical are indispensable to them! The realms of beauty and of worship established themselves apart, and fashioned their own special rites and language, and their own sentiments and pieties. And it inevitably followed that our *duties* took on a corresponding restriction and reduction.

Yet how can the Gospel conserve and renew its essential power unless it copes with the whole man and with the whole of life? It flourishes only as it encounters man where he is and lives.

The dualism in question is above all a misunderstanding with regard to the Holy Spirit. We tend to think of the Spirit as a mood or a blessing that has to do with the top story of our natures, and most often in detachment from life. But it is rather an energizing and purging of our whole creaturely and practical being, involving all our natural and moral relationships.[5] In this sense we should say that God's Spirit does not come *down* but comes *through*. It does not give us escape *from* this world but solutions *within* it. Our misunderstanding of God's "Word" is similar. We see it as a bolt from the blue or a light shining suddenly upon the soul or an impact of the Absolute or of the Wholly Other. Thus we give due recognition, indeed, to the divine initiative. But too often we fail to recognize that the Word reaches us through our wrestlings with very mundane and ordinary experience.

Everyone will agree when we say that religion should not be separated from life. But many do not realize what this involves. They think it merely means

[5] Cf. Théo Preiss: "We ordinarily think that it is only the soul of man which is touched by the action of the Spirit, when it is the entire man who is affected because the whole man, soul and body, will be resurrected." "The Inner Witness of the Spirit," *ibid.*, p. 274. See discussion, pp. 273-75.

that we must not go outside the world like hermits or "mystics"; or that we must not just be Sunday Christians. But it means a lot more than that. It means more than that we can serve God in the office and the kitchen. The Reformation taught us indeed that our secular vocations must be looked on in terms of religious vocation. Many Christians will recognize this but they still separate religion and life in a deeper sense. They see their lay calling as one that requires honesty, sobriety, philanthropy and charity. But this is not the point. The common idea is that God speaks to us in church or in prayer, and that we are then to do his will in the secular life. But what we should recognize is that God also speaks to us precisely in our secular experience; finds his way to us in and through all our natural relationships. If he is blocked here he cannot speak to us very significantly in church.

A man's real religion or irreligion develops out of his experience with the things that are truly important to him as he comes of age: such things as his tension with his elders, achieving acceptance with his fellows, locating his particular talent, coming to terms with military service, getting married and earning a living. It is in wrestling with such dilemmas that he has the best chance to discover God, whether in success or failure. The church must not let these important private dramas go on outside its purview, unguided and unblessed. Likewise with the grown man and woman. There are large tracts of their experience which the church only blesses from a distance. We have in mind here, for example, the sense of meaninglessness that many men have in their jobs; or the false ideas of social status that are found in the village as well as in the suburb, which so confuse our sense of values and make the lives of so many men and women petty from beginning to end. Religion is falsely spiritual unless it engages itself with all these kinds of provinces in the private and the public life.

III   There are two supporting considerations that may be offered in connection with this charge that modern Christianity is guilty of a false spirituality and deals with only a part of life and a part of man.

On the one hand note the analogy of the arts. The situation of traditional art among us is a perfect analogy of the situation of religion. Traditional art has long accepted the role of alien or exile in the modern world. Aaron Copeland, the composer, states the matter well in connection with music.

In a Philistine world a great deal of music has perpetuated the tradition in a safe detachment from the Babel of our materialistic civilization.[6]

[6] *Music and Imagination* (Cambridge: Harvard University Press, 1952), p. 107.

Historical factors have brought it about that all the arts in this period have suffered under this limitation of belonging to a somewhat private world.

Traditional art is separated from life, and not merely in the sense that it avoids dealing with diesel engines, jet planes and miracle drugs. It may deal with these. It is separated from life in the deeper sense that it identifies itself with a special realm called Beauty, and with sentiments and themes of a particular kind considered to be artistic. Thus traditional poetry has its own restricted vocabulary, its own approved rhythms and cadences; its own cherished moods of magic and elegy. Even when it treats of evil it speaks from the ivory tower. There is a split in experience. The poet is only part of the man. A considerable part of life experience has been surrendered over to prose. Art becomes, as we say, inspirational; meaning that it is thought of in terms of either thrill or solace. So the average man has come to look upon it. The parallel with religion is disturbing. The most damning thing about traditional art today is that so many look on it as marginal, decorative, optional.

Of course much traditional art, much Victorian and prewar poetry for example, is invaluable and lasting. But it labors under the long historical handicap of which we have spoken. It was conceived and born in a dualistic culture, in an age which forced art off into a corner. The new arts, whether poetry or painting or music, are refusing to accept this split in experience. Modern art tolerates no false idealism or spirituality. It does not propose to be inspirational in the narrow escapist sense. It moves toward incarnation, the total man, our total experience.

What I have been summarizing here is the accepted understanding of the predicament of the arts and the humanities in the twentieth century. The analogy holds for the Christian Gospel. For the same historical forces have been at work in either case. Both art and Christianity have been made to appear marginal, unreal, unrelated. If we are to commend art to our time it must come down off its pedestal. If we are to commend the Gospel to our time it must emerge from the shrine and accept its own law of incarnation.

The whole matter can be illustrated in connection with popular religious painting. Take for instance the devout pictures familiar to us on the walls of our church schools and in our devotional literature. On the one hand we recognize how much hallowed Christian sentiment attaches to them for many believers. These pictures, as we say, tell a story or propose a lesson or create a mood. We respect or should respect what our fellow Christians cherish, just as in the case of the old-fashioned Gospel hymns. But then we can ask questions. Does this inspirational art really search us or only soothe us? And granted that one proper role of religion is to soothe or console and help us to escape, does this art accomplish this in a deeply Christian way or only on the surface? And with regard to these pictures that teach a lesson: do they genuinely convict us or is it all too evident that they propose to propagandize us? Are they didactic in the bad sense?

In an article in the *Yale Divinity News* Mrs. Martha Goethals draws an excellent contrast between "calendar art" and prophetic art.

The symbols of popular Christianity such as Easter lilies, sunrises and sunsets, open Bibles and candles, are lukewarm. Most contemporary efforts to use images or visual forms in interpreting the life and religion of Israel rely primarily upon journalistic illustrations. Amos becomes a ruddy individual with a dirty beard who shouts woes and banishes the rich with shaking fist. . . . The feeling that art can "manipulate" or genuinely create faith may lie behind some of the so-called "religious" (Sunday School) art. This it seems to me is the folly of all propagandist, didactic art.[7]

On the other hand, "contemporary prophetic art," as she adds,

is the expression of compulsion. A friend wrote to the French painter, Rouault: "You paint as one exorcizes."

This is the point. Genuine art exorcizes, calls forth the true self and casts out demons. Like the word of God it is not lukewarm, but

[7] "Rouault: A Prophetic Artist," *Yale Divinity News,* June, 1953, p. 3.

living and active, sharper than any two-edged sword, pierc-
ing to the division of soul and spirit, of joints and marrow,
and discerning the thoughts and intentions of the heart.
Heb. 4:12.

But to do this art must address the whole man.

We have quoted Aaron Copeland above with reference to the safe detachment of traditional music from
the modern Babel. Such isolation, he adds, is no
longer possible. The artist must go the hard way of
grappling with what his age represents. It is one thing
to compose *in* an industrial era. It is another "when
industrialization enters the framework of what had
previously been our comparatively restricted musical
life." [8] Surely we may register the fact that today industrialization with all that it signifies, and many
other at first sight alien and intractable elements, have
entered the framework of our hitherto comparatively
restricted *religious* life. This sets new terms for Christian evangelism.

Christianity like modern art must take its materials
from the stuff of life, ugly and dangerous though
much of it is. The sculptor may work in alabaster but
a Michelangelo can make nothing of a block of Car-
rara marble unless he has first wrestled with Floren-
tine humanity. Dante traverses all the circles of Hell
to know what Paradise means, and his Hell was not a
private one alone but the inferno of a whole age and

[8] *Ibid.,* p. 107.

of many cities and courts. T. S. Eliot's great achieve-
ment rests on the fact that he has himself been initiated into the furies and stagnations of our age and its
cities. The language of Eliot is not an idealist language. It is not, fortunately, an angelic, an uncontami-
nated, an immaculate language. Both the artist and his
language have to be baptized in reality if they are to
be effective. Let the theologian and the preacher take
note.

IV   The second consideration that we wish to offer
in connection with this charge of false spirituality in
our faith is the whole character of religion as we find
it in the Bible and especially in the Old Testament.
We have noted that our idea of religion short-cuts a
great deal of our human nature and our primary human relationships. This is certainly not true of the
Bible. Here God makes himself known where men
really live, in concrete circumstances, and not to a
part of a man but to the whole man. Religion in the
Bible roots in man's primordial impulses and social
bonds, and that is why it is powerful. In the Old Testament we see God at work as man seeks to solve his
basic problems of family and social life, and to give
order to the natural affections and vitalities with
which he was endowed. Religion here, as it ought to
be with us, wrestles with the powerful, intractable but

God-given raw material of human nature as it evolves new patterns in the family and the tribe and the nation.

Take for illustration the oldest strata of the Old Testament. Here we find a wealth of poignant and often shocking stores about the A, B, C's of human nature: in Genesis, in the Book of Judges and in II Samuel. Take the episode of the sacrifice of Isaac—father and son; of Hagar and Ishmael—mother and child; the recognition scene between Joseph and his brethren—brother and brother; the wonderful reunion in Egypt of Joseph with his old father Jacob—again, father and son; the immolation of Jephthah's daughter—father and daughter; David and Jonathan—comrade and comrade; or David and his mighty men who brought him water from the well of Bethlehem which was beside the gate—chieftain and servant.

These parts of the Bible are full of such vivid episodes, poignant little dramas of Everyman, in which the elemental relationships of life are spotlighted, and the instincts and passions that lie behind these. Why is this kind of material here in such abundance? It is not enough to say that here as in Homer we find a marvelous gamut of human nature portrayed. The point is rather this. The Bible recognizes that God finds his way to us, and we to him, through the deep primordial cravings, yearnings, loyalties, bonds, suggested by these relationships of parent and child, husband and wife, chieftain and follower. Here we find the raw material of revelation. Our theologians of the Old Testament today emphasize the great teachings of the prophets, or the conception of the Covenant or the over-all idea of the *Heilsgeschichte*, or history of salvation. But we should remember that all these rest back upon and are deeply embedded in the kind of concrete and intimate life experience reflected in the old stories. And the case is the same with the New Testament church though the writings here more often assume it. We must not separate our doctrine and theology from humble and obscure realities. The "hiding places" of religion's power are always to be found in the saga of the common life, and in the way God uses and crowns our creaturely endowments.

Let us look more closely at one of these old episodes, the atrocious story of Rizpah, the concubine of Saul. It will be recalled that two of her sons were put to death and impaled with five other descendants of Saul, at the behest of David and the sacred lot, to appease the Gibeonites and stay the famine.

And they hanged them on the mountain before the Lord, and the seven of them perished together. They were put to death in the first days of harvest, at the beginning of the barley harvest.

Then Rizpah the daughter of Aiah took sackcloth and spread it for herself on the rock, from the beginning of harvest until the rain fell upon them from heavens; and she did not allow the birds of the air to come upon them by day or the beasts of the field by night. II Sam. 21:9–10.

Here is savage vendetta on the third generation; here is a priest very possibly manipulating the oracle against the innocent; here is if not the crucifixion of the living at least an abhorrent exposure of the dead; yet here also is mother love against the sable background of error and cruelty.[9] The story despite the sobriety of its narration is overwhelming. Why is it in the Bible? What is its place in the historical books? What is its place in the *Heilsgeschichte?* We could ask the same question about the anecdote of David's homesickness and the heroic devotion of his three mighty men, two chapters later. Are these merely irrelevant episodes of sentiment, the one of mother love, the other of hero saga? Can we not find many similar tales among the annals of the Scottish Highlanders or the American red men, or in the *Iliad?* The point rather is that such stories disclose to us the subsoil of common humanity with which God is always wrestling; the roots of faith, doctrine and liturgy which must never be separated from their flower.

A corollary for today would be that vital religion must have its eyes open to what is going on outside the church in the common areas of adolescence, falling in love, family life, learning a trade, making a living,

---

[9] Cf. J. E. McFadyen, *The Interest of the Bible* (London: Hodder & Stoughton, 1922), p. 90.

love of country, and in such war experiences as com-
radeship in arms, endurance, heroism, horror and
treachery. The Spirit of God moves in unexpected
places. As Péguy said, "Grace is insidious. If it doesn't
come from the right, it comes from the left; if it
doesn't come from above, it comes from below. . . ."
We rightly value the offices of the church, the proclamation of the Gospel, the Word of God in Scripture,
as the vehicles of God's action. But behind all these
lies God's intimate commerce with the lives of men in
the ordinary experiences. We must have our eyes open
to his dealings in secular situations: amid the tensions
today between the older and younger generation; in
connection with the obstacles to love between the
sexes and the frustrations of marriage in our society;
and with the hurts and thwarting of youth as they seek
to solve their problem of security in the competitive
hierarchies of our economy.

Let us make one other comment on these Old Testament stories. It is worth noting that they deal with just
such material as we tend to make fun of as "sob stuff"
when we meet it in modern form. Mother love in
Hagar and Rizpah; pathos for the little lad (the
"sonny boy" motif); the "my hero" routine in connection with David; and "do-or-die" heroics. Of
course the stories in the Bible are not told in a sentimental way. But they have to do with these elemental
relationships and natural yearnings like mother love,

love of country and hero worship, which involve our very entrails. These stories lay bare the roots of human vitality, the cables which carry the powerful voltage of human impulse and action, whether creative or destructive. The modern psychologist knows how important these ingredients in our make-up are. Now the Bible evidently sees these drives, their satisfactions and thwartings, as God's opportunity. God works through these features of our creaturely nature. Here are the needs to which God gives answer. It is out of frustrations here, in part, that the prophet receives his call. It is thence that dreams and ideals take on power and elicit devotion. The tree of Judaism has its roots in these kinds of human realities. The vitality and meaning of the Messianic hope and of eschatology spring up from these explosive forces in our nature. We must not fall into an otherworldliness either liberal or neo-orthodox which neglects these potent resources of great faith.

We conclude then that the Bible is a very human book and warns against any kind of false spirituality or idealism. Revelation and the grace of God are tied up inseparably with our "somatic" existence, as we say today; that is, with our fleshly-sensuous-bodily life with all its organic relationships, widening out as these do into the social, economic and political spheres. God does not and cannot by-pass the original endowment with which he created us; nor the bonds

that link us with nature, family and clan. Any understanding of Christ or of the early church or of the
theology of Paul or of the message for today which
disassociates these from man's natural affections and
common needs is bound to be wrong. Any redemption
so offered us will not be a truly relevant one.

2

NEW TESTAMENT THEOLOGY
TODAY: A CRITIQUE

New developments in New Testament scholarship are of the greatest importance for an understanding of the Christian faith today. The results of a long period of biblical study are being put together in a constructive way so that we have a much better grasp of the nature of the New Testament church and its outlook. It is in this connection that we hear so much recently about the revival of biblical theology, and particularly about the *kerygma* or message of the first Christians. We have here a great resource not only for understanding Christianity but for commending it effectively to men of our time. Moreover, this new vital formulation of the Gospel runs across denominational lines and breaks down the walls between different historic confessions and denominations. In some quarters it is clearing the way for renewed contact between those we have called liberals and conservatives.

Yet the new kerygmatic emphasis is highly controversial as is evident in the discussions both of scholars and of theologians. Our concern here is to ask how these trends in New Testament study and interpretation bear upon our problem of making the Gospel relevant for our time. Do they help us to overcome the false spirituality and unreality of modern Christianity?

I   Let us first, however, make a general comment upon this whole matter of the historical study of the Bible. We have spoken in our first chapter of the chaotic situation that prevails in this country with regard to the Scriptures. Conflicts over historical and literary criticism have no doubt played a considerable part in this, and will continue to do so. We can hope today for some pacification of these older disputes. The new trends in our liberal scholarship should bring the parties closer together. As Martin Dibelius has said: "Form criticism reconciles the critic and the church." Moreover, we may sense a new irenic disposition among those we call "liberals": a wish to appreciate the concerns that are precious to those they hitherto disparaged as "biblicists," and a desire to avoid discourteous and unchristian polemic.

We live in a time that is sobering for all Christians. We should lift the level of discussion to higher ground. The old lines of battle between liberal and conservative have in some important quarters been dissolving, and this process can be furthered where both sides practice candor and respect, and speak the truth as they see it in love. The shocks and convulsions of today should high light what Christians hold in common and draw them together as in World War II Protestant and Catholic and indeed Communist fought side by side in the resistance movements.

Of course we must recognize that when old disputes over the Scriptures are reconciled new ones arise. We must also admit that historical-critical study of the Bible brings with it new elements of "scandal" in each new period. When we reflect on these hazards that the authority of Scripture runs in all generations it is a comfort to remind ourselves sometimes that

The Bible will take care of itself!

No doubt it carries with it liabilities and stumbling blocks of a fantastic kind for a literature which makes a claim of universality. No doubt the Bible often stands in the way of its own truth. No doubt the hindrances in the Bible are doubled and quadrupled by many of its interpreters, and its ambiguities, irrelevancies and archaic features sanctioned and furthered by those who appeal to it.

Yet the Bible will take care of itself!

No doubt the labors of the most consecrated and instructed students of the Scripture seem sometimes to achieve little. We are tempted often to exclaim: What avails the obscure toil of the scholar, what the sober plea and testimony of the historian, what even the lifelong immolation of the greatest of these truth seekers, over against the impenetrable sway of religious custom and the transmission, generation after generation, of uncriticized and distorted or desiccated faith?

Yet the Bible will take care of itself and will in the long run take care of its faithful scribes. Here too wisdom is justified of its children, and justifies its children.

Let us admit that much as we cherish the work of the scholar and the interpreter, the real foes of the Bible are not finally inadequate historical understanding of it, nor the passing of time and the consequent strangeness of the Word to the ears of new generations, though these are real handicaps. Nor are they the impervious conservatism of religious bodies, nor indeed on the other hand what may appear the profane dissection of the Word of God by unspiritual critics. Its only great foes are, wherever they are found, hardness of heart, irresponsibility, pride and scorn. It is these alone that can really render the Bible obsolete and choke the Word.

And let us recognize that, after all, the final and decisive allies of the Bible are neither the printer nor the translator, the colporteur or even the exegete. Its truly decisive allies, wherever they exist and under whatever disguises, are the hunger and thirst of men after righteousness and eternal life. Since these exist, the Bible notwithstanding and nevertheless, will take care of itself. And may we not go a step farther and observe that even the ways of pride and revolt bring men ultimately to this very hunger and thirst.

We shall therefore not be finally dismayed with the more obvious obstacles to the free course of Scripture. These no doubt require our best attention and commit us to the tasks of interpretation and clarification by all possible skills and methods. What is finally important is that through whatever clouds of error or partial knowledge, such as hang over all of us, the living God should disclose his new creation to us and remove us from folly, waste of spirit and the old Adam. The greatest service of the scholar will be in bringing together the man and the message so that the Gospel may speak most effectively to his condition and circumstances.

It is well from time to time that the nonspecialist should be reminded of the prodigious labors that are expended upon the biblical sciences and upon any and every realm of investigation that impinges upon the Bible. The avidity, the devotion, the exhaustive researches and investigations, decade after decade in every Christian land, testify to some deep instinct in Christendom for the importance of the specifically historical aspect of our faith. One thinks of the innumerable fields of inquiry; of the costly expeditions, surveys, excavations; of international and interfaith projects; of the accumulated data; of the tools of study: thesauri, lexicons and encyclopedias; and of the libraries, museums, foundations, institutes and journals. This tireless probing of the past, financed and staffed both from within and without the churches, seems to proceed from some profound sense in the West that the clue to its own self-knowledge and health lies in this direction, lies indeed in the Bible and the Bible story and the Bible lands. The dawn that arose in Palestine has still to unfold its greater splendors and the historian has his own necessary part in the dissipating of the shadows.

II   The work of the liberal biblical scholar from the eighteenth to the twentieth century has been largely a work of historical reconstruction. It has been a part of the work of the modern world, through philology, archeology and other tools and methods, to "recover the past" and to throw light upon the story of man's life in time. It has been part of the wider attempt to get behind unexamined traditions, and to surmount the largely unconscious level at which the mass of mankind live, looking neither before nor after.

Most of us were bred in this kind of Enlightenment

attitude. The enemy was to be identified with obscurantism, superstition, ignorance, dogmatism, with all the tyrants of the mind and the spirit. What was needed was to shed a pitiless ray of light upon error, to dethrone the false authorities that presided over social custom, especially religious custom. The most effective way to do this was by a re-examination of the past. If the great masses of men through the centuries have lived like sleepwalkers, going through the motions of their fathers, it was time for some men to awake, to shake off the collective spell. And so, especially from the eighteenth century on, both political and religious myths were attacked; the icy scalpel of intellect, that is, scientific method, was applied to all that men held most precious. Hence the warfare between science and religion. Hence the outcries of traditional Christianity against the iconoclasm of the rationalist and the higher critic.

Yet the total effect of historical criticism of the Bible has not been mainly negative. This impulse of honesty has given us a truer picture of the past and therewith a correction of our understanding of the faith. And this kind of scientific study must go on. The church must constantly stand under correction both of the fiery Holy Spirit of God and of the cold scalpel of human intelligence, and these two are not so unrelated as may appear.

Yet today we recognize that the study of Scripture has entered upon a new phase.[1] This is part of a general transition in the whole conception of historical work and indeed of science itself. We look back upon the typical historical method of the nineteenth century today and we note its limitations. Many disparage its ideal of objectivity, and observe that as men of faith they are not interested in mere historical "information." Under the sway of existential or pragmatic demands we are in danger of swinging over to a mood of complete indifference to history. As always at such times there is misunderstanding, alarm and bitter polemic. To many scholars the values of historical method and scientific rigor seem threatened, along with the priceless contributory disciplines which lead so precarious a life. Many laymen are uncomfortably aware that the Christian liberalism they have known and cherished is under attack.

But let us characterize briefly some of the alleged shortcomings of the older historical procedure, and connect these with defective views of the Bible to which they contributed.

We may dismiss the charge that the older-type historian was positivistic in his presuppositions. Some no doubt were. But the true historian while he sought

[1] Cf. W. Schweitzer, "The position of New Testament study," in *Biblical Authority for Today*, ed. by A. Richardson and W. Schweitzer (Philadelphia: Westminster Press, 1951), pp. 131–34.

natural causes for phenomena like any good scientist, left ultimate factors open. What we can say is that few of the historians of the nineteenth century give us the impression that they were very much aware of the dynamics and dimensions of life. This may explain the flatness of much of the representation of biblical life, biography and thought that came out of this period. The superiority of Albert Schweitzer over the students of the life of Christ and of Paul whom he canvassed can largely be explained by this one consideration.

The charge that orthodox historical method took the form of analysis rather than synthesis, that it cut up the great works of the past into ribbons and dismembered the Scriptures has a good deal of truth in it. In any case analysis had to precede synthesis. What we can hold against these historians is the kind of synthesis they did practice or assume. They usually thought like good Darwinians in terms of genetic origins and evolutionary development. When it came to the Bible this involved a delineation of progress in ideas and ethics. This offered a useful and defensible frame of reference for throwing into relief certain features of biblical religion. But it also tended to obscure others. These scholars were inclined to miss the importance of what they called "primitive" conceptions. Thus the early Israelites held a fascinating naïve and mythical idea of the unity of man and nature,

whose importance we are just beginning to realize.[2]
But to the liberal historian this was just superstition.
Similarly with biblical ideas of tribal solidarity, belief
in demons, eschatological myth, etc. We have now be-
gun to grasp the deeper importance of some of these
alleged naïve ideas. The same holds with early and
continuing cult practices. Another blind spot had to
do with the imaginative elements in ancient docu-
ments. These students looked for "concepts" in the
Psalms and in the prophetic oracles and by-passed
their significant mythopoetic features.

If we say that these scholars had too narrow a view
of historical objectivity we should be clear what we
mean. In one sense the historian cannot be too objective. What can be said is that they were not as aware
as they should have been of the subjective factors af-
fecting their views and of the inevitable relativity of
all judgments.

But a chief limitation of their historical method lay
in the rationalist presuppositions which were bound
to affect their conclusions. We can illustrate this in
connection with the older portrait of Jesus and the
early church. The whole approach encouraged, as it
were, a philosopher's view of the Gospel and the
Bible. The center of attention was given to the teachings or ideas of Jesus and the prophets, and to the

[2] Cf. Eduard Buess, *"Das antike Weltbild in der Bibel als theologisches Problem," Theologische Zeitschrift,* 1952, pp. 113–15.

moral ideals of Scripture. But the Gospels are not
textbooks of religious ideas and ideals and values.
They are dramas. The moment of revelation is found
there not as in a catechism or in a book on "how to
think positively." It is found as, by analogy, we find it
in the shock of discovery occasioned by some formidable life experience.

It is in this rationalism, this emphasis on ideas and
ideals, that we have one of the contributing factors to
the otherworldliness, the separation of religion from
life, of which we have spoken. The tendency on this
side has been for Christianity to be narrowly identified with religious concepts, right ideas about God,
religious truth. All this was an understandable but
unfortunate accompaniment of the immense contribution which modern rationalism brought to our understanding of man and his history. But the outcome is
that our contemporaries in this respect find Christianity doctrinaire and unrelated to life.

It is to be recognized that orthodox historicism
often supplemented the rational emphasis we have
described. Some students emphasized the life of the
religious group and its ritual practices, usually however after a descriptive fashion and without our more
recent awareness of the major significance of ritual
and myth. More general was the tendency to interpret
the religion of the Old Testament and the origin of
Christianity in terms of the religious experience of in-

dividuals, especially of the greater figures, such as the prophets, Jesus and Paul. Here a certain limiting presupposition drawn from the modern spirit was at work. The Hebrew prophets were thought of as great solitaries and innovators, and as pure individualists. The fact is, the prophets spoke in a cultic-institutional setting, and the form of their messages was given by tradition.[3]

But our strictures against the older generation of historians and biblical scholars should not be overstated. Those of us brought up and trained in the liberal tradition of biblical study can testify that historical criticism was carried on in a context of deeply Christian insight. Our teachers did not neglect the central matters of faith. Their method was influenced by prevailing semisecular ideas; rationalism, individualism, the idea of progress, the idea of religious experience. But on the other hand, by using such categories they were able to communicate to their contemporaries. Indeed, these ideas still have a qualified validity and certainly a wide currency, and the theologian and the preacher must still reckon with them if they are to be effective.

III   We turn now to a description of the changed

[3] Cf. E. Würthwein, *"Der Ursprung der prophetischen Gerichtsrede,"* *Zeitschrift für Theologie und Kirche,* 49, 1952, pp. 1–2, 8.

situation in biblical studies and interpretation that
has arisen during the last generation. We have been
hearing a good deal for some time of the "biblical revival," of the "new biblical theology," and of the importance of the *kerygma* for preaching and theology.
These terms do indeed indicate a genuine revitaliza-
tion of Christianity that is today under way. It is
potent both because it arises out of a better understanding of the Scriptures and because it speaks effectively to a new climate in our cultural life.

If a driving impulse of many throughout the nineteenth and early twentieth century was for emancipation from hardened custom by the operation of
intelligence, the widespread craving today is for spiritual security, for a revelation that will afford a real
sense of identity and a measure of freedom over
against the giant forces in which the modern man feels
himself caught. In this sense we can speak of a transition from a liberal to a postliberal period, though it
has quite a different character in this country from
that in Europe. In response to this new cultural craving biblical theology turns from its earlier liberal
themes to focus on the message of the post-Easter
church, the message of our deliverance through Christ
from this present evil age and from the tyranny of its
principalities and powers. The substance of this testimony was certainly not absent from the liberal faith
in which many of us were brought up. But today this

evangelical center of the New Testament is high
lighted. Our hesitations with regard to this new kerygmatic emphasis have to do with the narrow and literal
way in which it is often formulated. As we shall see,
it is again a question of this-worldliness and otherworldliness, and whether justice is done to both.

But we must characterize this new phase of New
Testament interpretation more fully. The changed situation is due to three new factors: (1) the more recent advances in scholarly work, (2) the demand of
the church upon the specialists for clear leads from
the Bible in a time of crisis, and (3) the influence of
the dialectical theology in conjunction with the modern mood of which we have spoken.

The scholarly advances which have entered into the
current New Testament theology are increasingly familiar to all of us. First, recognition of the importance
of the eschatological outlook of Jesus and the first believers. We not only see now how potent this mythology was in the formulation of the Good News. We
also see that it was part of their whole meaningful
view of God's working in history from creation to
judgment. The message was proclaimed by a church
that saw itself moving into the final stages of God's
glorious purpose.

A second major contribution lies in the area of
form criticism and all that is associated with it. We
learn here that the focus of interest and central dy-

namic of the early Christian community lay in the
story of Jesus not in and of itself, but interpreted as
the action of God. What we know of the early sermons
discloses this. We have had our attention called to the
content of the early preaching and confessions. We
have also come to see how the character of all our
Gospels was determined by this witness of faith, and
not only the Gospels as wholes but the oral tradition
embodied in them.

In the third place we have reached a better understanding as to the Bible's view of man.[4] And we can
see the validity of certain aspects of this view which
we might once have thought of as naïve. Thus man is
seen in his psychosomatic unity. The dualism of body
and spirit which we find in so much non-Christian religion and in so much romantic idealism is ruled out.
Again, man is seen in his social involvement. Here
various types of individualism are excluded. Finally,
man is seen as a historical being in the sense that he
necessarily participates in an ongoing process through
action, choices, etc. Here all ideas of salvation through
escape into a static inaction or contemplation are put
in question, whether Platonic or spiritualist. Man as
the Bible sees him lives in a horizontal dimension just

[4] Cf. G. Ernest Wright, *The Biblical Doctrine of Man in Society*
(Ecumenical Biblical Studies No. 2 [London: S. C. M. Press, 1954]).
Also, C. H. Dodd and others, *Man in God's Design according to the
New Testament* (Newcastle upon Tyne: Studiorum Novi Testamenti
Societas, 1953).

as he lives in a social context, and any perpendicular dimension he enjoys here or hereafter is conditioned by these aspects of his creaturehood.

On the basis of these findings and others in recent biblical study the scholars have been able to draw up constructive new presentations of New Testament theology. C. H. Dodd put the matter well in observing that the time had come in which a long period of scholarly analysis should give place to one of synthesis. Thus the conclusions of the specialists became available to faith in a sense that had not been true hitherto.

These constructive presentations of the early Christian faith and life take different forms. Some scholars confine themselves to a sober and largely descriptive method. But others present the material in a distinctly confessional form. Writing as Christians, speaking from faith to faith, they have produced what is rapidly becoming an extensive library of biblical theology: handbooks, commentaries, articles and special studies. The writers in question understand their task in terms of what is called "theological exegesis," meaning thereby an interpretation of the writings which can speak to us today directly as the Word of God. This work is often strongly stamped with the categories and terminology of the dialectical theology or of existentialism.

The characteristic theme of this biblical theology is

that God has revealed himself in a series of related historical episodes, all pointing toward his final purpose for mankind though at first involving a particular people. Historical revelation, election, covenant, community, eschatology, these are the key terms. This formulation in terms of *Heilsgeschichte*, the world-historical drama of salvation, is not new in biblical theology. What is new is its reappearance in the context of modern criticism. What it means from the point of view of the New Testament is best stated in terms of the content of the *kerygma*. The *kerygma* refers to the proclamation of the early believers that in Jesus' life, death and resurrection and in the giving of the Holy Spirit to the church, God, in accordance with the Scriptures, had been at work bringing in the new age whose final consummation would not be long delayed.

This understanding of the early Christian message has one great value for us today and one great liability. It safeguards the fact that the Gospel is a proclamation of good news and not merely a teaching of right ideas about religion. This good news, moreover, rests upon a once-for-all actual event in history. But there is one serious misunderstanding to which our reiterated reference to the *kerygma* leads: we get the mistaken impression that the preached Word is primary, as though the building up of the church were chiefly a verbal and confessional matter. On this basis it is too easy to separate, if we may put it this way, God's dealing with our ears from his dealing with our entire lives. What God did in Christ was more than to announce a message; it was to bring a new kind of community to birth, to effect a new social creation.

To be a Christian is something that goes deeper than our ideas and confessions and deeper than our code of behavior. It means our incorporation in a stream of history and in the redemptive events which determined that stream. It means belonging to a community whose members participate in a shared drama of the past, in a revelatory history. This is evidently more than a matter of hearing the cult story preached; it is a matter of sharing in the cult rite and in the total life of the cult community. To share in this *life* is to appropriate the revelation in just as real a sense as to hear it proclaimed. Thus too exclusive an emphasis on the *kerygma*, or even on "word and sacrament," tends to narrow the meaning of what it is to be a Christian.

The neo-orthodox emphasis in biblical interpretation has no doubt been of inestimable service to the churches abroad in recent years. It is an effective version of the Gospel in those quarters where men are already deeply versed in the Bible, and especially where Christians are subjected to perils and temptations of an exceptionally drastic kind which throw them back upon ultimate issues of personal decision. It is true that the question of final loyalty is one that

always confronts all Christians. But the new kerygmatic biblical theology as commonly formulated has
many limitations. It is biblicist in the sense that it uses
the terms and conceptions of the New Testament without adequate translation into modern equivalents.
Thus it can take on an archaic and wooden character
which, as Bultmann has shown, constitutes a very
poor apologetic method so far as the modern man is
concerned. Moreover, it too often presupposes a gulf
between the Word of God and the actual course of human experience. Despite its emphasis on our obedience to God in the existential moment, the claim of
God and the grace of God are not related to our duties
and our needs. The Word of God takes on a kind of
abstraction.

It is true that when one reads the exegetical sermons
that come to us today from the threatened Christians
of the East Zone of Germany, it is perfectly clear that
the church in such a situation finds supreme resources
in this kind of a Gospel.[5] But contacts with Christian
groups abroad and reading in the literature produced
by their Evangelical Academies, Church Assemblies
and other groups, lead to the conclusion that many of
these Christians are like many good Christians over
here. They have never really learned to think about
their religion in a social dimension. Many of their

[5] For example: Günther Jacob, *Das Licht scheint in der Finsternis;
Zeugnisse aus dem zweiten Kirchenkampf* (Stuttgart, 1954).

churches have a long tradition of political abstention behind them, and they tend to dismiss any kind of political realism on the part of Christians with such scornful phrases as "secular Utopianism," or "worldly opportunism." This black-and-white view of Christian social witness is related to the exclusively perpendicular way in which they understand the revelation of God.

We are not overlooking their heroic witness against totalitarianism. We also recognize that all genuine Christian commitment in one way or another influences the prevailing social and political forms. But we find that their idea of the political witness of the Christian confines itself too much to occasions when the church and the freedom of the Word are under attack.

One of the most damaging criticisms recently made of the current theological interpretation of the Bible is that of the veteran Swedish scholar, the late Anton Fridrichsen. He calls it "modern fundamentalism," "illusionism," and "a religious gnosis." Since a return to biblical literalism is no longer possible, writes Fridrichsen, there is but one way out for these new fundamentalists, namely,

to break loose from history and view the Bible as a purely metaphysical word, a document come into existence supernaturally.

But what results is

an illusionism which, though it recognizes that the written word falls short of conveying the historical reality with which it deals, nevertheless declares that everything depends on the word: history we must not search. That would be to let human thought sit as judge of God's revealed word.[6]

A similar warning is voiced by Professor Frederick C. Grant against the danger in much contemporary biblical theology; that

of treating that body of thought as if it were unrelated to history and were somehow suspended in thin air.[7]

IV   Our main purpose in this lecture, however, is positive and not negative. How do the new trends in biblical interpretation help us to speak effectively to the modern man?

I suppose myself now addressing the proverbial "secularist," a man we will assume to be of some education, who asks me to tell him what religion is all about, and who challenges me to show where Christianity today has anything to say to his problems and

[6] *En Bok om Bibeln* (Lund, 1948), p. 65; as cited in World Council of Churches' "Study 52/E112," July, 1952, p. 6.

[7] *An Introduction to New Testament Thought* (Nashville: Abingdon Press, 1950), p. 27.

his needs. He is a man pursued not so much by intellectual problems as by personal ones: family, job, security, status, etc. He may be a student soon to be mobilized; he may be in the air force in Korea; he may be a young businessman sensitive to the moral confusions all about him whether in the office or the country club; or a modern intellectual or artist initiated into all the nihilism of this period which Malraux calls the "aftermath of the absolute." Or it may be a young mother impotent to save a marriage that is breaking up, or harassed by her helplessness in what concerns her adolescent children.

Whoever it is, he tells me that he no longer goes to church. He finds no answer to his questions there. The minister says many true things but they do not touch him at the level where he has been seared or terrified or haunted. The people of the church are friendly; he is not superior toward them. But they have not been where he has been, or so he thinks, and they seem to respond to different signals from those he responds to. Phrases from the Bible register with him but he finds it a mystifying book full of archaic conceptions. Its message as interpreted by conservatives seems otherworldly; as interpreted by liberals it seems platitudinous or perfectionist. He has the impression he is being asked to shut his eyes and go on a religious jag by the former, or to haul himself up by his own bootstraps by the latter.

Now with a man of this kind the current biblical theology of the Word of God may well have a real appeal, just as Roman Catholicism may. The latter will offer him an authority and a "home" of a very objective kind. In fact two things are essential in any such option: something objective and commanding, and something that will engage the imagination. The Roman Catholic has both. The neo-orthodox can offer the objective and commanding message with something of the august about it, but he lacks the imaginative appeal, as naturally follows from his repudiation of culture and of the whole natural context and soil of faith.

But what both the Roman Catholic and the neo-orthodox lack is what I can only call a personal realism, a message to the man in his actuality, in his many-sided actualities: in his family relations, economic harassments, and psychological scars and maladies, as well as in what we call his spiritual need which is inseparable from all of these.

The orthodox will address him as a "sinner"; the neo-orthodox as a "creature"; the liberal, perhaps as a "soul." But the Bible properly understood will address him as a man: as a man and a son of man and a son of woman, and as a father and a neighbor and a citizen and a craftsman and a breadwinner.

And the "message" I would speak to such a man if he asked me what Christianity really meant and what there was about it that could make any meaning to him, would be something like this.

You, John Doe, misunderstand the Christian faith. You misunderstand the Bible and its claim. The enemies of Christianity have persuaded you that it is something irrelevant and escapist. The friends of Christianity have led you to believe that it is a matter of occasional high moods, thrills or aspirations; above the ruck and desperation, the incubus of fear or the nausea of your personal life; unrelated to the traps in which the individual is caught in the stony cities, in the lush but cynical suburbs and in the tyrannical towns.

But I can tell you that it is only in such harsh actualities and relationships that Christianity can be itself, correct itself and come to life. You are quite right in looking askance at any self-styled religion that only plays around the edges, that only concerns itself with your "soul" or your emotions or your capacity for mysticism, or even your troubled conscience. Religion is supposed to do more than any of these things; it is supposed to save! You are quite right in your demand that religion should take over the total situation in which you find yourself. To "save" means saving the whole man and not just his emotions. And it cannot be just an individual matter; the man must be saved in his relationships.

What we believers call grace is not just something

that meets us at the margin of life. It springs up like a fountain in the midst of life. We speak of the Holy Spirit as descending upon us and this is a proper figure of speech since it brings out the fact that it is God who is the giver of the Spirit. But as a matter of fact the Spirit doesn't so much come down as come through.

Grace, as the Bible understands it, takes occasion of human situations.

It is like fire that has to have fuel, and the fuel is life experience.

You, John Doe, are candid to confess that for your part you see life very much as a rushing back and forth in a trap, as a recurrent encounter with "no exits," blank walls. You do not claim to be innocent; in fact you are haunted with a sense of helpless responsibility and connivance in the monstrous daily toll of ruin that accumulates all about you. You have a right instinct in not wanting to be saved alone out of this tangled web of human miscarriage.

In the play "Agamemnon" by William Alfred, there is a scene in which Clytemnestra speaks of such a sense of guilt and of being forever removed from innocence.

> The picture in my mind of what I was
> Had, I don't know, grown dingy, I suppose. . . .

As if I had been crying in my dreams
All night on shuttered streets half-lit with stars,
Because I was a partner in some wrong,
In some default of faith 'too base for words;
And waking hoarse, should find the world I left
Swept still by clean-cut winds and cleansing light,
But somehow find it as a pauper child
Must find a trinket it can never own,
Heart-breaking in its beauty—Punished, I feel,
Resigned, yet in that resignation
Slow triumph like a blush, beyond mere joy,
Flows up through me; and all things are
Precious and distant, as in a brazen mirror,
And intricately small.[8]

The Bible is on your side, John Doe, in recognizing that any salvage operations for yourself and all the other prisoners, conscripts, robots, hollow men, ghost lives, and men and women generally in this "age of anxiety"—any salvage operations here cannot be effected by strains of ravishing celestial music or by invocation of a deus ex machina *or voice from heaven. It can only be effected by immanent creative and redemptive operations in the situation, in the "grass roots" or rather in the thicket and jungle of the common life: there where grace shows the other side of the same coin; where the fuel of the human lot catches fire from heaven; where the blank wall turns into a door.*

[8] William Alfred, *Agamemnon* (New York: Alfred A. Knopf, 1954), pp. 35–36. Used by permission of the publisher.

Therefore, what Christianity has to say today, John Doe, should make more sense to you than either the orthodox formulas or the noble liberal teachings which you have heard for a long time, or than the recent existentialist challenge to a total surrender. It is good news as always; but not merely an external assertion which so much of your experience belies. It is good news which is at one and the same time a persuasion from within. It is an unbelievable unaccountable irradiation of the dark places of our lives; a realization of the inexhaustible generosities of God at those precise points where there seemed to be only irremediable evil and hopeless obstacles.

Light breaks where no sun shines.[9]

The message to you then takes the form of a plea that you believe what you already believe! Namely, that the key to life's meaning and ultimate transfiguration is found in the Christian epic and the Christian drama and the Christian rite. The plea is that you prove, confirm this faith in your secular circumstances, as you are led, however baffling the conditions. The plea is that you take on responsibility for the new humanity, the new race of men, that is, the true church, the embodiment of this faith. The plea is that you link yourself up with the meek and the merciful,

[9] Dylan Thomas, *The World I Breathe* (Norfolk, Conn.: New Directions, 1939), p. 24.

and extricate yourself from the manias and intoxications of the age—especially from its false conceptions of status and acceptance, prestige and authority. It is a plea that you open yourselves to the leadings and charities of God where you are, in "the daily dust of life," no matter how low the ceiling under which you live, and no matter how full of violence and menace the theater of your action. And you will be given eyes to see his sometimes inconspicuous and sometimes formidable and open work of judgment and favor— or both at once—in the affairs of men.

It is in some such way that we can address the new kind of man that our age has produced, the secularist, the disaffected, using our new understanding of the Bible and trying to carry over its conceptions so that they will have meaning today. In the two chapters that follow we shall have opportunity to carry this further.

3

THE JESUS OF HISTORY AND MODERN DOCETISM

A great deal of modern Christianity reminds us of these orchids that are said to live on air. They bloom up off the ground and nourish themselves apparently on ozone. So it is with many Christians, including many "liberal" Christians: they live off of ideals and dreams which have very little to do with the rich soil and humus of everyday life. What is more, we tend to think of Jesus and the beginnings of the Gospel in the same way. Jesus was a kind of angel or myth, an air-nourished orchid who had little to do with "the daily dust of life." In the Far East the lotus is a favored symbol for Brahma or the Buddha. It is an immaculate bloom floating on the dark waters that has no apparent connection with anything mundane.

This damnable heresy which theologians call docetism, and which we may call a two-story view of life, keeps on recurring through the whole history of the church and plagues us all. Although we know that Jesus of Nazareth died on a Roman cross, involved in a charge of sedition, and that the origin of the church was a matter of divided families and social ostracism

—a matter of blood, sweat and tears—yet we insist on making poetry or theology of all this. We do not really grasp the fact that God's grace is mediated through actual situations. Though we read that Jesus wept over Jerusalem, as Jeremiah did at an earlier time, we cannot get it through our heads that in both cases this involved the perennial human yearning we call patriotism. No, we theologize it. We somehow cannot admit the fact that Jesus loved his country and his people as Joan of Arc loved her country, and we cannot see that this kind of human devotion played a part in "revelation."

As we have seen in our first chapter, it was through such natural affections and human loyalties in the earlier life of tribes that God found a way to disclose himself. And later the loftiest conceptions of Zion and the New Jerusalem and the Kingdom of God took on substance from them.

At one end of the story stands Moses calling upon Jahweh to destroy him in place of the people that he loved. And at the other end stands Paul, one of the deepest secrets of whose life is revealed in the following passage:

I have great sorrow and unceasing anguish in my heart. For I could wish that I myself were accursed and cut off from Christ for the sake of my brethren, my kinsmen, by race. They are Israelites, and to them belong the sonship, the glory, the covenants, the giving of the law, the worship, and the promises. ROM. 9:2-4 [1]

In between these two figures we have the cross of Jeremiah as he is torn between his tenderness and love for his people and the irresistible summons of God to cry, Havoc! The hardest thing for Jeremiah is that the Lord says to him:

Therefore, do not pray for this people, or lift up a cry or prayer on their behalf. JER. 11:14

and

Though Moses and Samuel stood before me, yet my heart would not turn toward this people. JER. 15:1

Is it not clear that the commanding force of either the prophetic or the apostolic witness in such cases is directly connected with their wounded love for their people?

God's dealing with the prophets was certainly not unconnected with everyday life. Our traditions link Hosea's grasp of God's forgiving love with his own heartbreaking experience of a broken marriage. Nor did God speak to Jeremiah "out of the blue" but in connection with the prophet's desolation at the evil courses of his kindred and his people. Are we to think of the calling and power of Jesus of Nazareth as unre-

[1] Unless otherwise indicated, scriptural quotations are from *The Holy Bible, Revised Standard Version* (New York: Nelson, 1952).

lated to vital issues of his day and to the deep sentiments and loyalties of a son of Israel?

In Anton Zweig's play, *Jeremiah,* there occurs the
following striking line: "The Lord cuts from the tree
of life him whom he hath chosen for a scourge." [2] So it
was with Hosea and Jeremiah, and so it was with the
Son of Man. Grace finds its opportunities in just such
bruised and lacerated hearts. It is through such human
brokenness and anguish that new light breaks, and the
vision of the redeemed Israel rises out of the ruins of
Israel rejected.

Professor Carl H. Kraeling in his *John the Baptist* [3]
has given us a persuasive interpretation of the way in
which immediate social factors conditioned a major
figure in the same generation as that of Jesus. How did
it come about that this youth turned aside from the
sacred obligation of the priesthood imposed by his
lineage to become a voice in the wilderness? The circumstances allow us to reconstruct a costly and
dramatic personal revolt. Kraeling traces it to his
"profound sense of revulsion" against the representa-
tives of the priestly calling.

He may well have been led to regard what he saw going on at Jerusalem as a desecration of a high calling,
jeopardizing the nation's acceptability before God and

[2] New York: Viking, 1929, p. 169.
[3] New York: Scribner, 1951. The three quotations that follow are
from pp. 26–27.

destined only to bring the wrath of a jealous God down
upon his faithless servants.

John's refusal of ordination

could well have rendered him quite unintelligible to the
simpler folk of his native environment . . . making life
equally intolerable for him there and sending him forth
in bitter anguish of soul into the wilderness.

We may well conclude that the growing tension between the young John and the worldly priesthood as
well as cruel cleavage with his family and neighbors
would have served to light up for him the deeper issues of his generation and thus mediated to him his
fateful message.

But Professor Kraeling appropriately invokes the
case of Jesus himself at this point.

The analogy here is to Jesus' own experience at the
fatal Passover, when the spectacle of the Holy City prepar-
ing to celebrate the Feast of the National Deliverance
without heeding his call to repentance and to national
consecration provoked his most violent acts, elicited his
direst prophecies and gave to his words the note of pathos
and sadness.

We make the Christ story unreal and we gnosticize
the Gospel unless we at least begin with a recognition
that Jesus was a Jew and loved his people and his land
and Jerusalem, the city of the great King. His patriotism was sublimated, indeed, and projected itself in
eschatological images, but its sources were in a senti-

ment common to our human nature. The salvation Jesus wrought had, of course, its transcendent and universal significance, but it had its base in his wrestling with the problem of his people in his generation. The cost of Jesus' struggle with false views of their calling and its basis in his own ardent love of country is well suggested in a poem of the New Zealand writer, Eileen Duggan, entitled "Nationality."

> Because He was a man
> As well as He was God,
> He loved His own goat-nibbled hills,
> His crumbling Jewish sod.
> He bowed to Roman rule
> And dared none to rebel
> But oh the windflowers out of Naim,
> We know He loved them well!
> He must have loved its tongue,
> His Aramaic brogue,
> As much as any Norman loves
> The accents of La Hogue . . .
> As heifers to their young
> Christ's bowels yearned to His sod—
> He was the very Jew of Jews
> And yet since He was God—
> Oh you with frontiered hearts,
> Conceive it if you can—
> It was not life alone He gave
> But country up for man.[4]

[4] Eileen Duggan, *Poems*, pp. 44–45. Copyright, 1939, by the Macmillan Company. Used by permission of the publisher.

So much by way of introduction. Our task in what follows is to reinforce out of the New Testament this theme that the great and valid otherworldiness of the Gospel has its roots in this-worldliness, and that this relation must ever be maintained.

I   If we are to commend our faith to men today and break through the unreality associated with it how shall we deal with the gospel story of the Christ?

Our problem is the age-old problem of doing justice to the Christ of faith without losing our hold upon the reality and humility of the Nazarene. From the beginning, indeed from the first writing of Gospels, the church has been so concerned with the transcendent significance of the revelation that it has obscured the original circumstances and actuality. Many will say today that any precise historical visualization of Jesus in the days of his flesh is not important. The first Christians saw him in terms of their faith, with the eyes of faith, and in this way safely transmitted to us what was essential as regards his historical life. This should be enough for us. There is truth in this view, and it is on this basis that the overwhelming majority of Christians have been blessed. But we live in an age when both the historical Jesus and the Christ of faith are widely misunderstood and when as in earlier periods an appeal to the original event in something of its circumstantiality is needed as a corrective.

It is true that liberal Protestantism has emphasized the historical Jesus and the social gospel, and here we have seen a significant leading of the Spirit. But the Jesus so presented was modernized out of all resemblance, and the scholars of that period were handicapped by the unripe state of gospel study. Liberalism most often failed to reckon with the fact that the Jesus of history was, as Albert Schweitzer made clear, a stranger and an alien to our day; that his thinking was not as our thinking, and his language not as our language.

We should not be too sure that Jesus of Nazareth, if we could have seen him, would conform to all the ideas we have about him. We may well take to heart the rather surprising hint that we get from a famous Old Testament prophecy which the church has always understood as a true prediction of him. It is rather startling that this passage, perhaps the greatest in the Old Testament, tells us that

he hath no form nor comeliness; and when we shall see him, there is no beauty that we should desire him. IS. 53:2 (A. V.)

Such a portrait does not fit well with many modern conceptions of Jesus. This surely need not be taken to mean that there was no glory of love to be seen in his lineaments. But was it the kind of loveliness which we

look for? Those whose ideals of beauty are drawn
from modern sentiment, from pre-Raphaelite paint-
ings or even from ancient Hellas, not to mention Hol-
lywood, might well find the genuine beauty of holiness
something of a disenchantment.

One may say that there are three misconceptions of
Christ widespread today, and each one conduces to
the sense of unreality felt about the Gospel by the
modern man. We have first the ethereal Christ of ec-
clesiastical art, the Christ of the stained-glass window.
We have, second, the sentimental Christ portrayed
with flowing amber locks and benign countenance. We
have finally Christ the myth, the "x" or unknown
quantity, commended not to the sense of sight at all
but rather to the ear as a disembodied Word.

Over against all these and some other portraits we
find a saying in the Gospels peculiarly relevant:

> And then if any one says to you, "Look, here is the
> Christ!" or "Look, there he is!" do not believe it. False
> Christs and false prophets will arise and show signs and
> wonders, to lead astray, if possible, the elect. MK. 13:21, 22

All in all, the liberal concern with the historical
Jesus represented a proper protest against the unreality and dogmatism of a great deal of fossilized Christianity. There was a true instinct here that the rightful
image of Christ in glory could only be recovered by
way of a realistic dealing with Christ in the flesh. A

false otherworldliness is a perpetual temptation of the church. Human nature has a fatal propensity for spiritualism, gnosticism, for either refined transports or violent orgies of the soul, which offer an escape from life, an opiate for its burdens or torments, or at best too easy a resolution of life's demands. We all crave for revelation, rightly. But we prefer one that will lift us off the earth, make angels of us here and now, and dispense us if not of the toil of our hands like the Thessalonians, at least of our duty to our brothers like the Christians in Corinth. And this is all the easier for us if we dissociate Christ from the moil and toil and welter of everyday humanity.

We find a revealing index of the church's struggle with this temptation when we consider the history of Christian art. This appears especially in the attitude of the early church toward the portrayal of Christ in painting and sculpture.

Until the fourth century A.D., we find no Christian art in the sense of representational art. The symbolic-decorative work of the catacombs and the sarcophagi and the souvenirs of pilgrimage do not qualify here.[5] This is understandable since the whole effort of early Christianity had been directed against pagan idolatry and images. Moreover, artists were generally classed

[5] Cf. Hans von Campenhausen, *"Die Bilderfrage als theologisches Problem der alten Kirche,"* Zeitschrift für Theologie und Kirche, 49, 1952, 36.

with actors and keepers of brothels as men whose pro-
fessions identified them with heathenism and its cor-
ruptions. Near the beginning of the fourth century,
however, we have the record of an interesting episode.
No less a person than Constantia, the sister of Constantine, wrote to Eusebius of Caesarea asking him to
secure for her a picture of Jesus. Eusebius in reply
points out how misconceived such a portrayal would
be. Hans von Campenhausen thus summarizes his
reply.

A picture of Christ *in his divine aspect,* is of course out
of the question and would contradict the express prohibi-
tion against making an image of God as everywhere obeyed
in the Church. But even a picture of Christ *in his human
manifestation* is out of the question. For already in the
days of his flesh he was so irradiated and swallowed up
with divine glory that the disciples could not endure to
look upon him on the Mount of Transfiguration. Thus it
would be altogether impossible to portray him with "dead
and lifeless paints." [6]

And von Campenhausen adds:

These opinions demonstrate in a naïve and consistent
way the same trend towards the reduction of the human
in the person of Jesus as had appeared earlier more
crassly in the docetism of Gnosis and later in a more refined way in the monophysite Christology. The mortal aspect is irradiated, transfigured and swallowed up by the
overmastering power of the heavenly glory. This is the

[6] *Ibid.,* p. 38.

basic tendency of the Christology of the entire ancient Church, or, rather, a basic danger with which it had always to wrestle. . . . According to Eusebius, Christ was "born like unto us and clothed after the fashion of mortal man, yet not indeed as man, but God." [7]

The historical Jesus went into eclipse in varying degrees in the early centuries because of the gnosticizing character of early Christianity, which was fascinated by wonderful conceptions of metamorphosis and deification.

In later centuries the representation of Christ in art was, of course, finally justified and carried out with varying theological presuppositions. Where a doctrine of the two natures of Christ prevailed the portrayal of his humanity was defended, though always exposed to the charge of Nestorianism. The main stream of Byzantine and Orthodox Christianity through its icons has striven "to set forth the invisible Christ through the visible without betraying the invisible." [8] Its emphasis on transfiguration and apotheosis, based on the Johannine writings, inhibited any interest in mundane particulars. Its concern with man's primary sense, that of vision, enhanced the role of the image but reduced the importance of history.

On the other hand Western sacred art has in certain periods offered realistic portrayals of the Naza-

[7] *Ibid.*, p. 39.
[8] *Ibid.* (citing Von Soden), p. 56.

rene. Both St. Francis and Dante exhibit powerful motifs drawn from the Jesus of the Synoptic Gospels. Western Christian theology, for its part, stressed the atoning death of Jesus rather than the incarnation of the Word. It stressed the sense of hearing rather than the sense of sight; the hearing, that is, of the Word spoken *in history*. It therefore was disposed to take the Jesus of history more realistically. Yet, as we know, both Western Christian art and theology have often lapsed into one or other form of docetism and unreality.

II   Having in mind, then, the heresies ancient and modern in the presentation of Christ, let us turn back to the original question. How can we today do better justice to the historical Jesus without obscuring his true significance, indeed, so as better to define the full significance of Jesus Christ? How does our recent New Testament study help us to take more seriously the meaning of incarnation?

We begin by admitting that our older liberal portrait of Jesus must be revised radically. Its gospel criticism was inadequate. Its presuppositions were often secular in the sense of rationalistic and individualistic. We have learned to see Jesus in terms of Jewish eschatology. We concede that the picture of Jesus given to us in all four Gospels was shaped by the early Resurrection faith rather than by an objective historical interest as *we* understand that.

The new biblical theology has this in its favor that it insists on the historical character of the revelation in Christ. Great stress is laid upon the saving event in history. Jesus was crucified under Pontius Pilate. The Christ story is not to be understood as a myth. The truth is not a matter of ideas and values. If we place ourselves upon the ground of the New Testament, we are not henceforth permitted to confuse Christianity with pantheism, idealism, mysticism, or with some proposed Esperanto religion for all nations based on universal ideas of truth, goodness and beauty. God is adequately known only in connection with an unrepeatable historical episode, related to a series of such episodes in the story of Israel. Christian faith has these particular roots. It is a tree that has grown in the Holy Land and not a rosy glow in the atmosphere of the soul. Salvation is of the Jews.

Yet in saying these things, New Testament theology today does not say enough. We cannot indeed deny the authority and effectiveness of much kerygmatic preaching along these lines, whether over against the Nazi challenge in the thirties or over against a secularized Gospel generally. But this kind of a message tends to abstraction. Its strength lies in the fact that it confronts men with the Word of God. It places men before the Cross in a kind of naked encounter. But it abstracts from the full humanity of Christ and it abstracts from the full realism of our response.

Let us put three alternatives this way:

1. The man Christ Jesus preached by neo-orthodoxy is a kind of symbol "x," an unknown quantity. It is insisted that there was a historical event and figure there, but all the emphasis falls upon what faith did and does with this "x." Christ is preached, not Jesus Christ. This leads to unreality.

2. The man Christ Jesus preached by the old orthodoxy is a supernatural figure, a God, or God himself. The truth of incarnation is acknowledged but not taken with full seriousness. Again, Christ is preached, not Jesus Christ.

3. The man Christ Jesus as preached by much liberalism has been a modernized prophet and teacher who gives us back our own best ideals. The full significance of the redemptive drama is missed. Here Jesus is preached, not Jesus Christ.

What other option do we have? Does not criticism today veto any biography of Jesus? And even any assured sketch of his career and teaching?

Much of this caution is required. But what is unjustifiable and even perverse is to conclude therefore that revelation has very little to do with the Nazarene in his concrete actuality. Even when God's Word is recognized as the Word of the Cross, the death of Jesus is abstracted in such a way that its setting in human circumstances is ignored—except as an irrelevant technical problem for the historian of religions.

The fact is that though we cannot write a biography of Jesus, and though we do not know assuredly, for example, how he thought of himself, yet the Gospels offer us the dependable outlines of a historical drama in the life of Israel. The terms and outcomes of the drama clearly locate and define the central figure. The operation of God is to be studied in the fateful conflict involved, and in the new community that emerged; and not in some bolt from the blue. We must exclude here the *deus ex machina,* and recognize God at work in the whole concrete transaction. The significance of Jesus, whether as Christ or by whatever other title, is to be studied in the social-historical human situation, which is by no means undocumented for us, and not resolved for us in terms of some metaphysical or theological status bestowed upon him from beyond the situation.

Our concern with the historical Jesus must not be misunderstood. We are not trying to go back to an old liberal view. It is not a matter of documenting the historical career of Jesus in any considerable detail, or arguing defensively for the historicity of disputed sayings or episodes, or offering a lame vindication of certain old sources, or of painfully drawing inferences together to prove, for example, that Jesus thought of himself exactly as the later church and the evangelists

understood it; that is, as Messiah, Son of Man and
Suffering Servant, all three at once! We do indeed re-
pudiate some of the extreme skepticism voiced with
regard to the records. But our main concern is to recognize a measure of human reality, indeed of sociolog-
ical reality, in the figure of the Nazarene; to identify
a real protagonist in a real this-worldly drama; to in-
vite attention to a realm of second-causes in the working of God; and so to arrest the impulse to docetism
which otherwise has a free field for itself.

When we speak of "the historical Jesus" objection
is made that the early Christians and the evangelists
were not interested in his historicity as we use the
term. They could take it for granted that he had ac-
tually lived. For the rest they give us interpretation
and meaning. As Professor Bo Reicke says:

The Synoptists were not interested in "historicity" in
the secular sense; otherwise they would have supplied us
with much richer biographical material. But what we
mean by historicity meant for them not something objective but above all something final. They did not think of
the life of Jesus so much as something past, or of his
actual existence in a given place and time, but much more
of his mission and task. . . . In this way the Synoptists
contemplate his historical existence basically under the
form of incarnation.[9]

We may accept this. But once we have observed what

  [9] "Einheitlichkeit oder verschiedene 'Lehrbegriffe' in der neutesta-
mentlichen Theologie?" Theologische Zeitschrift, IX, 1953, 410–11.

the interests of the evangelists were, we may have our own very good reasons for asking questions that were not primary for them. And fortunately they offer us material to which we can direct our questions though they did not look at this material in the same way. But the main point is that the historical Jesus was of absolutely crucial importance for them, though under a different angle of observation. We have every right to convey to our time in this connection what they conveyed effectively for their time. In their own way, together with their view of the Nazarene's eschatological significance, the evangelists give us a very real figure in his real setting, and along with it a sense of how important this was for them.

III   The Gospels abundantly evidence the fact that the drama which centered in Jesus of Nazareth concerned the calling and mission and promises of Israel and their frustration and miscarriage. It had to do with a broken covenant (though Jesus probably did not use this term), with a stewardship unfulfilled, and with a people envisioned as a fig tree barren of fruit. The son of Joseph was no "x" nor an icon in a niche, nor a Kierkegaard in advance of his time. He was a protagonist and actor in God's greatest controversy with his people. We meet with this theme of God's controversies with his people in the prophets and the

Psalms. It always involves indictment, call to repentance, and pronouncement of judgment on temple or nation. These arraignments of Israel stand in relation not only to hours of imminent peril for the nation and for Jerusalem but also to abuses against humanity and disloyalty to the covenant.[10]

Jesus, like Jeremiah, was animated by love for his land and people and he appealed to his generation in terms of Israel's heritage of vocation and hope. We have to do here with life, not with catechisms and dialectics. The ordeal of the Son of Man involved what we would call politics, no less; though politics in a very special form and with a prodigious background and scope: party politics, social cleavages, national goals and international attitudes. Of course, in Jesus' time politics was conceived of in theocratic terms. Government and economics and cultural life and religion were all one. Thus Jesus' message was both political and religious at the same time: a call to repentance, a challenge to corrupt institutions and authorities, and a compassionate action directed toward the neglected and the victimized of his day. He was, indeed, concerned with the eschatological new age to come, but in his context this meant no lack of realism

[10] Cf. Hos. 4:1 ff.; 12:2 ff.; Isa. 3:13 ff.; Mic. 6:1-2; Jer. 2:5 ff.; 25:30 ff.; Mal. 3:5. See Ernst Würthwein, "*Der Ursprung der prophetischen Gerichtsrede,*" *Zeitschrift für Theologie und Kirche,* 49, 1952, 1-16.

as regards the actual historical situation of his people. It has been said of Robert Frost that "his minute particulars run out into great universals." If we find great universals in the utterance of Jesus we should not sever these from the very concrete particulars, the life situation of his ministry.

We may illustrate from the case of John Brown. Comparing lesser things with greater we have here also a witness to eternal truth that rises above the centuries; but we have also a very concrete web of circumstances out of which this witness arose:

> John Brown, thou rock of iron in the stream
> Of man's facilities; obtrusive "nay"
> Flung at the world's abandonments; thou "stay"
> Out of the eternal, thrust up in the way
> Of custom's, season's, time's complacent "yea." [11]

The significance of John Brown's witness and "afterlife" in the American nation would be radically obscured if he only became a myth for us and if we lost sight of the circumstances of his action. In the same way God cannot speak to us through Christ unless we know who he was!

Consider now Jesus' parable of entrusted funds, that is, the parable of the talents, as we find it in Mt. 25 and in Lk. 19. In Matthew's version the third servant received one talent, "and he went and dug in the

[11] "As Sheep without a Shepherd," in the author's *Arachne: Poems* (New Haven: Yale University Press, 1928), p. 57.

ground and hid his master's money." In Luke's version one of the ten servants laid away his master's "pound" in a napkin. By an excusable homiletic extension—already initiated by the evangelists—we interpret this grudging, dog-in-the-manger policy in a moralizing sense. We see Jesus rebuking the individual who does not put his gifts to use. But Jesus, in his actual life situation as Martin Dibelius notes, was here accusing "the Jewish *people* who do not know how to use the precious heritage entrusted to them by God." [12] C. H. Dodd takes the same view, in effect.

Who is the servant of God who is condemned for an over-caution amounting to breach of trust? I would suggest that he is the type of pious Jew who comes in for so much criticism in the Gospels. He seeks personal security in a meticulous observance of the Law. He "builds a hedge about the Law," and tithes mint, anise and cummin, to win merit in the sight of God. "All these things," he says, "I have observed from my youth."—"Lo there Thou hast what is Thine!" Meanwhile, by a policy of selfish exclusiveness, he makes the religion of Israel barren. Simple folk, publicans and sinners, Gentiles, have no benefit from the Pharisaic observance of the Law, and God has no interests on his capital. . . .

"The Judaism of that time," says Dr. Klausner, "had no other aim than to save the tiny nation, the guardian of great ideals, from sinking into the broad sea of heathen culture?" Put that way, it seems a legitimate aim. But

[12] *From Tradition to Gospel* (New York: Scribner, 1935), p. 255.

from another point of view, might it not be aptly described
as hiding the treasure in a napkin? [13]

It is in this sense—that of an accusation of unfulfilled stewardship—that we can understand other sayings in the Gospels:

Is a lamp brought in to be put under a bushel, or under
a bed, and not on a stand? MK. 4:21 [14]

But woe to you, scribes and Pharisees, hypocrites! because you shut the kingdom of heaven against men; for
you neither enter yourselves, nor allow those who would
enter to go in. MT. 23:13 [15]

Woe to you lawyers! for you have taken away the key
of knowledge; you did not enter yourselves, and you
hindered those who were entering. LK. 11:52

[13] *The Parables of the Kingdom* (New York: Scribner, n.d.), pp.
151–52. Cf. B. T. D. Smith, *The Parables of the Synoptic Gospels*
(Cambridge, England: University Press, 1937), pp. 168–69. Dodd's
citation from Klausner is from the latter's *Jesus of Nazareth* (New
York: Macmillan, 1925), p. 376.

[14] Cf. Dodd, *op. cit.*, p. 145. Dodd sees the same original sense in
the saying about the salt which has become useless, p. 142.

[15] It is true that the Gospels misread the attitude of Jesus to the
scribes and Pharisees. The Matthean discourse assigned to Jesus in
Mt. 23, for example is affected throughout by the bitterness of the
Jewish Christians especially, and distorts his views almost beyond
recognition. (Cf. Ernst Haenchen, "Matthaus 23" *Zeitschrift für
Theologie und Kirche* 48 (1951) 1, pp. 38–62.) Yet we can penetrate
back behind Matthew's discourse. Where Matthew means that the
synagogue prevents and forbids Jews to enter the Christian Church,
Jesus in his situation rebukes the scribes for unchurching the "sinners" and otherwise failing to let the light of the Torah shine, and
for taking away the key of knowledge.

In all such sayings and parables Jesus was dealing with the miscarriage of the stewardship of Israel and speaking in the forum of his people's life. We are not surprised then when we find him also *acting* in this forum in the episode we call the purification of the temple.[16] It is altogether likely, moreover, that he used his own version of the classic parable of the wicked husbandmen in the last crucial days, although not with its present Christological conclusion.

But there is another line of thought which reinforces this view of the realism of Jesus' errand. The symbols that he used in appealing to his generation were not theological abstractions. They were the flags and banners of his people's hope. They were like torches and fuses calculated to ignite the aspirations of Israel. If his word and deed searched and convulsed the hearts of those that heard him, it was not because he spoke general religious truths, nor because he mediated an encounter with the Wholly Other at some timeless level. It was because in this fateful moment of his nation's destiny he invoked its supreme memories and loyalties. He exploited their relevant traditions by appealing to the great prototypes of the past and to the potent images of the national destiny. He

[16] Cf. John Marsh, *The Fullness of Time* (New York: Harper, 1952), pp. 114–15. "The exclusiveness of Israel meant in effect that the treasures of her religion, instead of being taken to all the nations of the earth, were being hoarded up for her own use and enjoyment."

lived all this out, chose twelve disciples as a sign of the gathering of the people, and reactivated the prophecies by symbolic words and deeds. Without involving the ambiguous figure of the Messiah he nevertheless invoked the supreme conception of the Son of Man coming to judgment as well as those of the New Temple and the Messianic Banquet.

In Rudolf Bultmann's *Theology of the New Testament* we find a forthright expression of the view of Jesus' message which we are here questioning.

Jesus no longer speaks, as the ancient prophets did, of the revelations of God in the history of the Nation and the nations. And when he refers to the coming judgment of God, unlike them he is no more thinking of catastrophes in the affairs of nations than he expects God's Reign to be fulfilled in the erection of a mighty and glorious Israelitic kingdom. Unlike the prophets' preaching, his preaching is directed not primarily to the people as a whole, but to individuals. . . .

Thus, Jesus in his thought of God—and of man in the light of this thought—"de-historized" God and man.[17]

Of course we must recognize that Jesus did not expect God's reign to be fulfilled in the erection of a mighty Israelitic kingdom. But in his theme that Jesus dehistorized God and man and "released the relation between God and man from its previous ties to history (history considered as the affairs of nations),"[18] in

[17] New York: Scribner, 1951, p. 25.
[18] *Ibid.*

this theme Professor Bultmann would seem to be giving us an abstraction which hardly does justice to the matter, the design without the coloring. The transcendental and dualistic images that Jesus used represented, indeed, a universalizing and deepening of older conceptions, but they were still redolent of Israel's theocratic ideals and took on their vitality from these.

His summons represented a real alternative to Jews a generation before the catastrophe that fell upon the nation and which cast its shadow before. The kingdom he proclaimed to individuals was defined by their corporate hope. The judgment and salvation he announced were inseparable from the story of the past and the real choices of the hour.[19]

[19] We should not be misled by Jesus' word to Peter as recorded in John 18:36: "My kingship is not of this world." The sense of the passage as Bultmann paraphrases it is: "My kingship does not have its origin in this world and so is not of this world's kind." (*Das Evangelium des Johannes* [Göttingen, 1950], p. 506.) The sequel offers the positive side of the teaching: Jesus' kingship—that of one who was born and came into this world from above—is the kingship of truth. It is clear that we have to do here with Johannine categories, decidedly removed from those which the Nazarene himself used. When we return to the Jesus of history we find, indeed, that he distinguishes between the things of Caesar and the things of God, and he proclaims the kingdom as an eschatological affair. But this is not otherworldliness or dualism in the Johannine sense. Jesus repudiated the worldly hopes and methods of Zealot agitators and their chauvinist Zion as he did the political or theocratic worldliness of the Sadducees. But his alternative was not for all that otherworldly. His idea of the new age for all its transcendental character and imagery gathered up all the hungers and aspirations of prophet and psalmist

Thus we conclude that it is not enough to say with the theologians that God acted in a historical event. We must give that event some concreteness and assign the actor flesh and blood. God moves in a mysterious way, we say. God acts "over our heads," that is, in ways that escape our recognition and confound our wisdom. All this is granted. But that does not mean that we should not trace his hand in his mighty works. In the gospel story God wrought through a tangled skein of political, social and very human circumstances. If we forget that this is what incarnation means we will evacuate faith of half its significance here and now.

In the early part of this chapter we have called attention to the artistic representation of Christ as a clue to our fundamental problem. We conclude by an example in recent art which suggests the direction in which we should look for a genuine encounter with the humanity of Jesus in all its revelatory significance.

Professor Heinrich Vogel of the Humboldt University in East Berlin has recently written his homage to the Swiss painter, Willy Fries, in an article entitled "Behold the Man." [20] Here is a painter who brings the scenes of the life of Christ right down into

and the devout poor looking toward the age of peace and righteousness and a new Temple, a house of prayer for all peoples.

[20] *Sehet den Menschen: Ein Fingerzeig zum Verständnis der Kunst von Willy Fries,*" *Theologische Zeitschrift,* 9, 3, Mai-Juni, 1953, 217–23.

our midst, as though we were present, as though we were seeing a cinerama moving picture. This is not just the Christ story "in modern dress"; it is something much more gripping than that. Thus the Annunciation takes place amid the ruins of a bombed German city, and one can recognize the towers of Munich's Frauenkirche in the distance. The flight into Egypt is pictured in a wintry Alpine gorge. Joseph and Mary bending over the child in a snowstorm might well be the hunted refugees of our cruel today. In the crucifixion scenes Christ hangs on a great beam in the uniform of a common soldier of World War II, sharing and redeeming the lot of so many of these years.

The painter himself explains his purpose.

The public has not always liked it when I have shown Pilate or the High Priest pronouncing sentence upon the Savior in our own familiar village square. It may also have made them uncomfortable to behold the Easter angel announcing the Resurrection in a snowy Alpine landscape in early spring. And what are these modern steel-helmeted soldiers and mockers doing at the foot of the cross, who only yesterday paced our streets and declaimed their pet [Nazi] views in our taverns? Or these modern sophists who were so clever in our classrooms?

What I wanted to do was to confront the observer and myself with our common guilt, face to face with Christ; as Max Picard warned us against "Hitler in ourselves." *Tua res agitur!* It concerns you and me! Above all, not to lay the guilt on others. The only one who can carry that crushing burden is the Man of Sorrows.[21]

Here is a clue, then, to the way in which the historical Jesus can be made truly contemporary. He was not a phantom. He was not an angel. He was not a myth. He was a flesh and blood Jewish patriot through whom God spoke and acted at the crossroads of history. God wrought salvation through him for the centuries and the continents just because he lived a real life amid real issues.

[21] Pp. 218–19.

4

THE RESURRECTION FAITH AND
A RELEVANT SALVATION

A religious message has real power only if the words
it uses are alive. The words must be "loaded"; they
must carry a charge. They must strike down into the
actual contemporary hungers and dreams of men. A
religious message has power only if its images and
symbols are important and alive. They must be like
flags or banners which command and quicken the ar-
dors of men. They must be like fuses or sparks in a
magazine that will ignite the latent energies of men.
We have seen what effective images could do even
when abused in the cases of fascism and communism.
These examples teach us in any case that human devotion is mobilized only when the symbols speak to
contemporary aspirations, however confused these
may be.

Now the words and images used by Jesus, Peter,
Paul and John had this character. They were not abstractions. They were not worn-out battle cries or
slogans. To talk about the Kingdom of God, the Messiah, the Savior, was to use words that were banners
and fuses and sparks. And the power behind these

terms was that of long accumulated social hungers and dreams. If the fulfillment of these dreams pointed also beyond this world that is because man is born with eternity in his heart. But we should not let ourselves be blinded to the fact that the real dynamic of the early Gospel arose out of the common life, and a long history of questing, suffering and conflict.

Our difficulty today is precisely that the words and images of the New Testament have become empty for many. They are not like banners or fuses. They do not as a matter of course strike down into the living needs and issues of life today. They do this, indeed, for those who have received Christian education, but even here only in a partial way. This does not mean that we must discard the language of the New Testament. But we must interpret it and relate it to the hungers of men today, both personal and social. The symbols and sacraments of the faith mean much in the house of worship but they will wither and be stifled there unless their original vital relation to all men and to the public secular life of all men is constantly refreshed.

I   We turn first to the Resurrection experiences and the Resurrection faith of the earliest days. Can we not get behind the unreality which obscures this crucial witness of the New Testament for many men today, and suggest its roots in the life situation of the first disciples? Here, indeed, it would seem that we stand face to face with the sheer divine miracle, the breaking in of the otherworldly power of God. But we can understand his work more and not less fully, if we can trace at all the second causes through which he wrought.

Now let us grant that the preaching of the Resurrection will always meet with incredulity in the world as it did when Paul spoke on Mars Hill. Nevertheless, a great deal depends on how we present it. What we need to do today is to Christianize our understanding of the Resurrection. If we tend to secularize our celebration of Christmas today, we do the same with Easter. Our purpose in these great festivals is to honor Christ, but we tend to render him pagan honors. In our understanding of the Resurrection we do not assign him the glories that are rightfully his. Pagan ideas of *apotheosis* tend to substitute themselves for Christian views of *resurrection*. We think of the Resurrection of Jesus more as the deification of a mortal, a sheer pagan wonder, without any particular relation to his love and obedience or to the redeemed humanity of which he is the first fruits. What we may call the apotheosis view isolates the Resurrection of Christ from its moral context and from the whole drama of salvation in which we are all involved.

We must make an effort here to put ourselves in the place of the first Christians. Their eyes were opened to the glory of the Crucified; they encountered their Master in his glory. They found the full meaning of this event in the prophecies, and in their radiant expectations of the New Age. The Resurrection was, therefore, for them the immediate prelude to the redemption of man and of nature, the final overthrow of Satan.[1] It was not an isolated event but part of God's final new creation. For the creation itself was to be delivered from bondage and there was to follow the manifestation of the children of God and the redemption of their bodies, as Paul describes it.

We do not wish to be misunderstood. The early Christians stood face to face with a wholly inexplicable wonder of God in their encounters with the glorified Christ. We still recognize this wonder when we are led in worship and in life to see the Lord in his glory. But what we would maintain is that this wonder and this glory are rooted in God's dealing with men in their everyday life. The Resurrection experience of the first disciples had its context in very human dilem-

[1] To use the language of biblical theology, the Resurrection of Christ had its setting in eschatology and Heilsgeschichte. As F. C. Grant says: ". . . the Resurrection was the beginning, in full earnest, of the 'coming' of the divine kingdom, and would be followed presently by the parousia of Christ in glory, the last judgment, and the inauguration of the New Age—all this is presupposed or reflected in the earliest sources we possess for primitive Christianity, and is taken for granted throughout the New Testament." *An Introduction to New Testament Thought* (Nashville: Abingdon Press, 1950), p. 228.

mas, in issues of the time that had a long background, in efforts to understand God's calling for his people, and in personal conflicts of loyalty and disloyalty. And for us too, a vital Resurrection faith is similarly relevant to our daily life and the great issues of God's will for mankind today. True experience of the Lordship of Christ is not a matter of theology but of life, and comes to us also as the solution of struggles in our generation to make sense of the world.

At this point we may find the current emphasis in biblical theology lacking in reality. These interpreters invoke the *kerygma*; including the testimony that Christ died, was buried, and rose again the third day according to the Scriptures. They often seem content to proclaim this as the Word of God without great concern to interpret it. The assumption seems to be that it is simply a matter of belief or unbelief. The revelation involved will grip those whom God elects. But we must show that the initial Resurrection appearances were integral to the needs and hopes of the first disciples, and not merely in a "spiritual" sense.

Now Rudolf Bultmann has sought to give meaning to the Resurrection of Christ for modern men in a much discussed proposal. He is far from depreciating the initiative of God and the supernatural character of the event. He places the emphasis upon the Cross itself and upon our own participation through repentance in the final obedience and death of Christ. Those, he says, who consent to be crucified with Christ awaken with him to God's new creation. They recognize his Resurrection *at one and the same time* that they themselves rise to newness of life. That Christ rose from the dead was and is revealed to faith alone, not to the unbelieving. Thus, on this view, *the Resurrection is the other side of the Cross when the Cross is looked on in faith.* Jesus on the Cross *is* Christ in glory for those who have eyes to see. Jesus on the Cross has already triumphed over all hostile powers, including death itself. There is much in the New Testament that supports this view. Bultmann calls especial attention to the Gospel of John, according to which Jesus is to be glorified when he is crucified, when he is "lifted up." But this interpretation appears also in the Epistle to the Hebrews, and underlies even the old traditions in the Book of Acts.[2]

The great value of Bultmann's view is that he refuses to allow the Cross and the Resurrection to be for us an external spectacle. We must identify ourselves

[2] With respect to Hebrews, F. C. Grant writes that the probable view of this author is that "the resurrection and ascension were identical, one and the same act, and that this act took place in the transcendental realm, unseen by mortal eyes; it was by his death that Jesus entered into the holy of holies of the temple not made with hands (9:11), or—in the figure used earlier in the book—'ascended far above the heavens, where he sits enthroned in glory at the right hand of God.'" *Op. cit.,* p. 229. Cf. A. N. Wilder, "Variant Traditions of the Resurrection in Acts," *Journal of Biblical Literature,* LXII, 1943, 307–18.

with them in faith, by dying and rising with Christ ourselves. The common objection to this view is that it allows for no Resurrection event in and of itself, apart from the Cross. In the context of our theme in these chapters hesitation arises rather with respect to its existential and otherworldly formulation. The conception of revelation and faith involved removes the operation of God in this supreme event too far from human and historical factors.

We cannot here go into the complex problems raised for us by the Resurrection narratives in the Gospels and in I Corinthians. The question as to the nature of the Resurrection body of Christ is both a formidable crux of dissension among believers, and a matter of scandal to unbelievers. Two remarks are, however, in order. First, let us have charity in our disagreements. If the issue of heresy arises here at all, do we not locate it in the wrong place? The real heresy is not a question of the kind of body that arose, though some Christians will always feel that all that is most important hangs upon this. Any real heresy, here as everywhere in the Christian faith, has to do with the Christian substance of our view, whether we interpret the matter after the world's standards or after God's: as those who are "in the flesh" or as those who are "in Christ." Christians may hold what we call "liberal" or "conservative" views about the Resurrection of Christ. In either case if by the Holy Spirit they recognize that here God approved and vindicated the way of obedience and love, the way of the Cross, the way of the Servant; and that here God's love and power were mediated for the continuous salvaging of human life by this same way, there is no heresy. If we must invoke heresy, it will be in connection with views either "liberal" or "conservative," which dissociate the great stupendous wonder from the love of God and of man, and which base faith upon a mere arbitrary fiat of omnipotence or see in it only a symbol of nature's periodic renewal.

Our second remark is that we should keep in mind the different world of conceptions in which men of that time lived and thought. We should not feel bound by the details of their outlook. In their own way the first Christians affirmed that the world order was not a finished creation. The concern of the New Testament with the miracles of healing, the control over nature, the resurrection of the body and the renovation of the earth, all testify that God is concerned with the redemption of our creaturely condition, body *and* spirit, and with our given humanity and the created order in which we live.[3]

[3] Ph. H. Menoud, *"Wunder und Sakrament im Neuen Testament," Theologische Zeitschrift,* 8, 3, Mai-June, 1952, pp. 168–69. The eschatological wonders evidence the fact of the restoration of God's sovereignty in his creation, which had been usurped by Satan. "The so-called nature miracles signify that in the kingdom of God nature will no longer represent a power often hostile to men in the fallen

Thus the earliest and fundamental element in the Resurrection witness of the New Testament church was the recognition of the glory of the crucified Jesus as a pledge of the great renovation of the world. In keeping with their Jewish views they interpreted Christ's victory in terms of the resurrection in one form or another of his "body," just as their wider hope included the transfiguration of nature. For their whole outlook tolerated no dualism of body and soul, nor of matter and spirit. Christ was therefore looked upon as the first fruits of those to be "raised," and the Christians of the first century looked forward to what Paul called the "adoption" of their bodies, *i. e.*, their transfiguration, in connection with the coming of the new creation.

Let us then suggest three steps in the early Christian thinking about the Resurrection of Christ.

1. The affirmation that God had raised Christ from the dead was a deduction from the vision of him in glory. They beheld his glory and knew therefore that he had been exalted by God.

2. The vision of Christ in glory came as the ripening and blossoming of their insight into the meaning of his life and teaching and death, no doubt furthered

---

creation. For man is created in the image of God to reign over the creation. A miracle like that of Jesus' walking on the sea, for instance, signifies by anticipation the restoration to man of his lordship over nature."

by their searching of the Scriptures. In the shadow and horror of the Cross the real significance of his whole career flashed upon them. Their eyes were opened to see what God had wrought in him, and who he was.

3. But this true meaning of his life and death had to do with the frustrated calling of Israel, with the anguishing problem of how God would or could still fulfill the promises, with the hopeless dilemma of God's covenanted people, as it faced destruction under the Romans.

The followers of Jesus during his earthly ministry had known that his cause had to do with the national hope. It is a true picture when we read in the Emmaus episode that the discouraged Cleopas exclaimed: "But we had hoped that he was the one to redeem Israel." It was because of this hope, which was both religious and political, that the disciples had been drawn to him, including one or more from the Zealot party. It is not surprising that the tradition includes references to the patriotic ambitions of the sons of Zebedee. But the national hope of the Jews had its various levels of conception, all the way from the most secular to the most devout. Jesus' outlook and method at first disappointed and finally completely bewildered the inner circle of his followers. It was not that his program was irrelevant to history and "escapist," nor that it denied the mission of Israel. He chose twelve disciples to signalize the national scope of his work. He deliberately dramatized the great sign of the Messianic Feast in the episode we call the "Feeding of the Multitude." He brought the great issues of his task before the authorities of the nation at the climax of his career. What disoriented his followers, rather, was the "way" he went, the way of the Servant, the way of the Cross, and his refusal of all ostensibly effective methods for redeeming Israel in that hour. The crucifixion at first appeared to them the logical and final catastrophe for any such attempt to solve Israel's problem.

The awful shock of the Cross, however, predisposed them to new impressions. The vision of Christ in glory came to them as the blossoming of an insight into the meaning of his whole career. His work had had to do with the hope and stewardship of Israel, the constitution of a renewed and holy Remnant, qualified to receive the promises and to enter into the New Age. The Resurrection experiences, therefore, meant that the disciples beheld the crucified Jesus in glory, both as the Son of Man seated at the right hand of God, and as the designated Lord of the messianic community, the new Israel. They were now able to recognize that "it behooved the Messiah to suffer and so to enter into his glory." The Resurrection experiences and the insight into the meaning of Jesus' career went together.

So for us also the recognition of Christ as Risen must be not a matter of accepted dogma but our own discovery, through wrestling with the main dilemmas of our time, that he is the living Lord of conscience and the Lord of history.

II So far we have spoken in rather general terms about the context of the Resurrection event. To deal with this more adequately we should get down to cases, and try to understand the initial Resurrection appearances in biographical and human terms in connection with witnesses like Peter and Paul. For this we have all too little in the records. Yet we have hints and clues.

The appearance of Christ to Peter was the first of all the appearances. This was a main factor in constituting him both leader of the early Jerusalem community and apostle to the circumcision.[4] We cannot exaggerate the importance of this appearance since in all likelihood it was causally related to the other appearances. Of this Luke 22:32 gives a hint: "and when you have turned again, strengthen your brethren."

Can we connect the great moment of Peter's insight and encounter with Christ in glory with life-situation factors that may illuminate it? The inner dynamics of the event could only be understood if we knew the full story of his personal relations with Jesus. The au-

[4] Oscar Cullmann, *Peter* (Philadelphia: Westminster, 1953), pp. 58–65.

thentic glory of the Crucified broke over the shattered disciple after he returned to his toil by the Sea of Galilee. There, according to the account in John 21, the risen Christ questions his love three times. As Cullmann says: "The threefold protestation of his love for the Lord and the threefold charge ("Feed my sheep") stand assuredly in deliberate contrast to the threefold denial." [5] We have two further clues. After his denials we are told in Luke 22:62 that Peter went out into the courtyard and "wept bitterly." A more revealing index of the circumstances appears, however, in Jesus' warning to the overconfident disciple on the occasion of the Last Supper:

Simon, Simon, behold, Satan demanded to have you, that he might sift you like wheat, but I have prayed for you that your faith may not fail; and when you have turned again, strengthen your brethren. LK. 22:31-32.

Thus the factors that went into Peter's encounter with the risen Lord surely included this very human one, the tug of war in his heart between loyalty and disloyalty and the opening up of the bottomless depths of terror in his soul in the consciousness of his default and its consequences. But even in death the "faithful Witness" could not leave Peter long in this extremity.

His spirit lives; he died and is alive,
That pure will haunts this guilty world forever.

[5] *Ibid.*, p. 60.

> How could men's idle fury drive
> That mighty Shepherd from his sheep? Or sever
> His heart from Mary's, Peter's? Or deprive
> Iscariot and the thief of his blest rod,
> Far in the ultimate night apart from God?
> Never, never
> Could death's thin shadows dim that ardent Sun! [6]

But this is not all. The temptation to disloyalty was also conditioned by a tug of war in Peter's thinking; confusions in his mind as to the cause to be served and as a right understanding of the hope of Israel. His threefold denial of his Master was related to his uncertainty with regard to Jesus' way and method. He had never been able to accept fully Jesus' understanding of the national hope and how it should be furthered. As long as this disciple saw the vocation of Israel and the messianic promises in terms of thrones and status and rank, it was impossible for him to recognize the victory of the Cross and the glory of the Crucified.

Likewise in the case of Paul we can fairly conclude that the experience on the road to Damascus centered in a growing clarification of insight as to the true calling of Israel and Jesus' place in it. To this problem of Israel's election and mission the earlier life of Paul had been zealously devoted. The human preparation

[6] "Alive for Evermore" from the author's *The Healing of the Waters* (New York: Harper, 1943), p. 35.

for the moment in which Christ appeared to him in glory was constituted by Paul's attempt to come to terms with the apparent frustration of his people's calling and promises. We have a poignant parallel to his case in that of a Jew who lived a little later, the author of Fourth Ezra, who pleads with God for some understanding of the destruction of Jerusalem and God's abandonment of his people, and (note the special relevance here to Paul's case) the hopeless condition of the Gentiles also and the fate of the world as a whole.[7]

Some such view as to the meaning of the Damascus experience is the clear conclusion today after more than a hundred years of study of the conversion of Paul. The seventh chapter of Romans is no doubt in part autobiographical but it is not the best guide to us in seeking the antecedents of the Damascus episode. Recent study has shown how inadequate is any psychologizing interpretation of it which connects it primarily with Paul's sense of guilt. Paul proceeds from this experience to proclaim Jesus as the Christ because his mind and heart have been illuminated to see in him the solution of the problem of Israel, in its relation to the Gentiles. As C. H. Dodd has written:

Sustained attempts were made to show that Paul's the-

---

[7] Cf. Gosta Lindeskog, "The Theology of Creation in the Old and New Testaments," in A. Fridrichsen *et al.*, *The Root of the Vine* (Westminster, England: Dacre Press, 1953), p. 12.

ology was spun out of his experience of conversion on the Damascus road and the "visions and revelations of the Lord" which ensued. . . . But such attempts were doomed to failure.[8]

Dodd goes on to show that Paul, like the other early Christian preachers, based his theology upon his understanding of "the mighty works of God," that is, upon the story of Jesus as seen in the context of the whole history of God's dealing with Israel and mankind. The appearance of Christ to Paul was related to a sudden insight into the true meaning of recent historical events. His eyes were opened to the true import of God's work in his generation. As in the case of Peter, the Resurrection appearance to Paul crystallized a long struggle to understand the world and God's ways with it.

The case is not finally so different with ourselves. We also acknowledge and confess Christ—in various ways, indeed—because in one fashion or another, at one time or another or at many times, we have beheld his glory, because he has manifested himself to us. But such experiences are not abnormal or esoteric. He does not manifest himself to us in an arbitrary fashion or "out of the blue." To us also as in the cases of Peter and Paul he discloses himself and his reign in connection with our struggle to make sense of the world and of our lives. He reveals himself as an an-

[8] *According to the Scriptures* (New York: Scribner, 1953), p. 134.

swer to our needs, and not only our private personal needs but our common needs. Thus he is revealed to us not only as "My Savior" as in a great deal of old-time religion but as "our Savior"; and not only as the Shepherd of the flock of the church, but as the Lord of history; as King of kings and Lord of lords.

Our discussion of the Resurrection and the Resurrection faith has thus sought to obviate here also the sense of unreality that clings about the Gospel. We have tried to show here again that its otherworldly dimension roots in very concrete this-worldly realities. Only if this connection is safeguarded are the great horizons of faith vital and healthy. The gulf between the Jesus of history and the Christ of faith is not so wide as is often proposed. It is true that revelation is here of the essence. "Flesh and blood has not revealed this to you, but my Father who is in heaven." But revelation did not act and does not act in a vacuum.

III We turn now to the titles given to Jesus. What did the first believers call him, and why? Such terms as Christ, Savior and Lord have lost their original sense for many today. As a result they have become vague tokens of honor, and that is perhaps why they lend themselves so easily to cursing and blasphemy. We can be sure that they meant something more precise at first. These appellations accorded to Jesus were, indeed, titles of honor, but they were much more than that. They were first of all interpretations of his role, of what he had done and was doing. When the first believers acclaimed Jesus as "Messiah" they were identifying his *function* rather than his status, his function as the bringer of salvation. It meant that he had enacted an expected historical role in Israel, a role of deliverance which was still to be completed.

These titles, Messiah, Son of God, etc., were not ascribed to Jesus as mere honorifics, as one would decorate or flatter royalty. An analogy appears in two ways we have of speaking of George Washington. If we call him a "demigod" we merely apply to him a flattering honorific. If we call him "the father of his country," we accord him a title descriptive of his actual services and of the benefits we owe to him.

Now no doubt the first Jewish titles of Jesus, Messiah and Son of Man, were eschatological titles. In different ways they meant that in Jesus God was bringing the old age to an end and inaugurating a transcendent new state of things. But these ideas of the Messiah's work and the Kingdom of God had arisen out of age-old hungers and aspirations and were both this-worldly and otherworldly. The idea of salvation, as Professor F. C. Grant defines the Greek term used in the Bible, meant "the whole state of welfare or well-being of the people in right relations to God." [9]

[9] *Op. cit.*, p. 247.

The evils from which redemption was longed for included political servitude, economic oppression, and other
purely this-worldly conditions which were interpreted as
a present denial of the sovereignty of God. . . . Much the
same may be said of the "eschatology" of Virgil and other
Roman poets of the early empire.[10]

Thus in recognizing Jesus as Messiah the earliest
Christian brotherhood associated with him very real
this-worldly as well as "spiritual" deliverance. Very
human and tangible benefits of the Kingdom of God
had already been realized among them. It was not just
a question of the forgiveness of sins and of the con-
ferring of the Holy Spirit as an otherworldly blessing.
We should not think of the Pentecost experience of
the first believers on the analogy of a modern Bowery
mission. The task of the Messiah included that of saving his people from their sins, but he would also save
them from all manner of bondage and insecurity. The
work and reign of the Messiah had reference to the
whole order of the world. We must not understand
the fall of Satan as lightning from heaven in a purely
mythical and spiritual sense. Satan tyrannized over
both body and soul; and when demons were cast out
by Jesus or in his name, the benefits were not only
otherworldly. The earliest followers of the Way
looked for the return of Christ to accomplish his work
but they were already blessed on the human level, and

[10] *Ibid.*, p. 233.

already emancipated from certain aspects of the existing Jewish ethos (including various degrees of anxiety, tension and hysteria) and some of its social patterns. Despite hardship and obloquy the converts to the new Israel saw themselves already as beneficiaries of the messianic redemption in a very real here-and-now sense.

Later the Gentile church came to identify Jesus as Lord, Son of God and World Savior; by titles, that is, which had been given to the conquerors and rulers of the world, especially to the emperors. When such titles were given to Augustus, for example, they expressed the homage of the Empire to one who had ushered in a new world age of peace and concord throughout the entire civilized world, putting an end to the bloody period of civil war and anarchy. Jesus receives these same titles, and the analogy is not confined to titles. With reference both to Jesus and the emperor we have other common motifs: the epiphany of the Deity; the formal publication of the good news or *evangelion* associated with the advent or birthday of the Caesar; the heralding of the divine Prince of Peace and founder of the new age of felicity; and deliverance from this present evil aeon.

That these titles and ideas were ascribed to Christ does not mean a mere transfer of pagan honors. Nor, of course, were they understood in a secular political sense in his case. Their import goes much deeper.

With a right instinct the early church saw in Jesus the true answer to the yearnings of the ancient world and its peoples for peace and righteousness. Since the time of Alexander the Great, at first in the East and then also in the West, men had come to see in their rulers the source not only of temporal blessings but also of those religious satisfactions of which they had been deprived by the downfall of the city states and the de-thronement of their civic deities.

As in connection with the longing of the peoples for redemption, terms and symbols for the desired fulfilment arose out of the very depths of religion, so did this "earnest expectation of the creation" carry over these same terms and images at one time upon the Roman emperor and at another time upon the person of the Jewish prophet, and still later upon many another wonder-child of antiquity. It is an index of the profound impulse which characterized this period both religiously and politically that identical titles transferred themselves from older heavenly to newer earthly deities. This impulse by which a new Savior was adorned with old honors betrays the perfervid aspirations of this perhaps the most religious of all periods.[11]

When, therefore, such pagan titles as Savior and Lord were given to Jesus (as in the case of the earlier Jewish title, Messiah), these inevitably had what we would call "welfare" connotations, social and political

[11] Ernst Lohemeyer, *Christuskult und Kaiserkult* (Tübingen: Mohr, 1919), pp. 24-25.

connotations, in the ears of converts. The meaning and potency of these appellations went back to long accumulated social and cultural hungers and ideals. Such this-worldly connotations were, indeed, inseparably fused with yearnings for eternal life and personal redemption. The Christians transfigured the political images they used for Christ and his reign. Their citizenship was a "citizenship in heaven." Yet throughout the Christians offered a tacit challenge to the pagan and imperial ideas of world salvation, and this inherent rivalry became more and more overt. It reaches its climax in the New Testament when the familiar title of the emperors, King of kings and Lord of lords, is defiantly assigned to Christ in the Book of Revelation.

Why is it that the author of Luke-Acts protests so much, overmuch, the political inoffensiveness of the church? What did the early Christians mean when they used the Canticles of Luke with their references to putting down the mighty from their seats and exalting them of low degree, and their invocation of the Davidic hope that God's people would be delivered from the hands of their enemies that they might serve him without fear in holiness and righteousness all the days of their life? Why is it that the Gospels and other writings of the New Testament can appeal to such Old Testament prophecies as that of the time when the Temple would be called "a house of prayer for all nations," and anticipate the time when the followers of Christ would sit on thrones judging not only the twelve tribes of Israel (Lk. 22:30) but the nations (1 Cor. 6:2). Such expectations are not to be understood in a secular sense but neither are they to be given a solely otherworldly sense. This would be to misread the mythopoetic character of the formulations. Understood in their true sense they involve a challenge to the hierarchies of paganism.[12]

Thus the confession of Jesus as Lord and Savior, and the claim of Christ over the whole civilized world as dramatized in Paul's far-reaching missionary goals, represented a continuation of the hopes of prophet, Psalmist and the devout poor for the time when God's will would be done on earth as in heaven. Granted the eschatological outlook of the church, their hopes were human hopes based on the human needs of the age, though transfigured by the poetry of faith. They blurred and merged temporal and eternal hopes. Similarly, in pagan terms, Vergil, in his Fourth

[12] Lohmeyer writes concerning the passage, Phil. 3:20 ("But our commonwealth is in heaven, and from it we await a Savior, the Lord Jesus Christ") : "Granted that the term 'Savior' was a well-worn coin whose original stamp was almost rubbed out. . . . Yet it is worth noting that an image drawn from political life (i. e., 'commonwealth') appears here in conjunction with the idea of Savior. This combination was actualized on earth only in the person of the Roman Caesar. The Roman citizenship on earth whose head was the imperial Savior stands here opposed to the citizenship in heaven of the Christian believers who are only waiting for their Savior Jesus Christ, and his continual presence in their midst." *Op. cit.*, p. 28.

Eclogue, provides "a message of hope and consolation to a sorely troubled world," announcing in 40 B.C. the deliverance of the world from its burden of "unrelieved fear" (*perpetua formidine*), under the coming reign of the young Octavian, but closing with the portrayal of a Golden Age, beyond history as we would say.[13]

It is true that the early church looked for the imminent parousia of Christ. This was an inevitable aspect of their picture of history. But this cannot set aside the fact that the believers were shaping a new pattern of human community and realizing very concrete social values in a widening movement which collided increasingly with existing institutions and vested interests, economic, social and political. In the second, third and fourth centuries, the church developed expressly the theme of the universal reign of Christ over the nations. It applied to him Vergil's oracle concerning the wonder child destined to bring in the Golden Age, and to be the Savior and Prince of Peace. Constantine adopted this view of Vergil's prophecy. This political interpretation of Christ as the universal *basileus* or king had its precedents in the messianic expectations of Israel and the Christology of the New Testament church.[14]

[13] H. J. Rose, *The Eclogues of Vergil* (Berkeley: University of California Press, 1942), pp. 162–63.

[14] Cf. Günther Bornkamm, "*Christus und die Welt in der urchrist-*

We do not mean to deny the otherworldly aspects of redemption hungered after in the mission field of the apostles: especially rebirth into eternal life, into the incorruptible existence of the gods. We find this yearning for immortality in various forms, in the Orphic mysteries, in late Stoicism and in Neo-Pythagoreanism. Among the Jews also the older sense of corporate life had broken down and the individual Jew had been led to make his claim for resurrection. The idea of salvation in the Christian message gathered up these yearnings of the age, both Jewish and Greek, and gave them a substantial answer.

Thus to call Jesus "Savior," whether as Lord or as Son of God, suggested deliverance from the foes of mankind both in this age and in the age to come. In this world it meant deliverance from very concrete ills and burdens, such as sickness, the assaults of demons, insecurity, and what Bultmann calls the "spiritual malaise" associated with astrology, fate and magic.

The titles of Christ and the idea of salvation in the New Testament had very concrete roots in the cultural and political life of Israel and of the Roman Empire. The terms in which the Gospel was presented geared in to the contemporary hungers and aspirations of men, both this-worldly and otherworldly. The supernatural life of faith was inseparable from everyday

lichen Botschaft," Zeitschrift für Theologie und Kirche, 47, 1950, 2, pp. 212–19,

human matters. The pyramid of early Christian eschatology and otherworldly hopes rested upon a broad base in first-century social and political actualities.

The Christians of the first century were not the otherworldly fantasists and ascetics that we sometimes think they were. They saw themselves, indeed, as pilgrims and they suffered various forms of social persecution and in rare cases martyrdom. But they had a better life on the whole than their contemporaries, Jews or Gentile, because of their group life and mutual aid,[15] and because of their emancipation from old social tyrannies. The rest of the world for a large part lived under a low ceiling that dwarfed and stifled personal values. The this-worldly satisfactions of the church are reflected in Jesus' prediction:

Truly, I say to you, there is no one who has left house or brothers or sisters or mother or father or children or lands, for my sake and for the gospel, who will not receive a hundredfold *now in this time*, houses and brothers and sisters and mothers and children and lands, with persecutions. . . . MK. 10:29-30.

* * * *

The conclusion of these chapters can be briefly stated. "Time makes ancient good uncouth." The doctrines and patterns and symbols of Christianity were

[15] Cf. Bo Reicke, *Festfreude und Zelos* (Wiesbaden: Harrassowitz, 1951).

at the beginning vitally related to the main currents of life. In our time they have lost something of this immediate relevancy. We may illustrate by the predicament of the British monarchy today as dramatized by the coronation of Queen Elizabeth. The ancient ceremonies no doubt had power to stir deep levels of sentiment and loyalty in the hearts of the people. But the institution of the monarchy itself is only partially related today to the crucial issues and determinations of policy. The changing configuration of real power and real interest empties the significance of the crown to an appreciable degree, and to that extent the drama and the coruscations of the rites take on an archaic character.

The analogy holds with institutional Christianity. It is imperative that the Gospel, both community and mission, be replanted in every age at the crossroads of human concern and die to live in new and relevant expressions. But in our age changes in the world and its thought have outrun the adaptations of the faith. Too many, perhaps without realizing it, have come to think of the Christian life as necessarily having a private character. As a result some of the crucial moral and spiritual issues of today have to be fought out largely in secular terms. Those who call themselves liberal Protestants have always been aware of this danger of letting the forms of the past isolate us from the living needs of the present. But we also have our own ways of taking up a position at a remove from the main engagement.

The Gospel speaks to us of peace with God and eternal life; but we are constantly tempted to isolate these from their original biblical setting in the turbulencies of actual society.

The church has always been subject to the temptation to divert the great stream of grace by a private conduit into a special preserve, into an institution or institutions, or into special patterns and usages. The imperative necessity of such forms beguiles us into an unwarranted and fateful fixation of the forms. Even where the rightful claims of continuity and universality speak for such conservatism, vigilance with regard to the changing climate of the generations should lead us ever again to scrutinize our situation. Rites and formulations once potent in their appeal to men may lose this appropriateness. The religious life then becomes isolated from the common life and takes on the character of a false legalism or false spirituality. In the course of time the stream of grace once effectually mediated through these forms begins to fail and faith is no longer greatly nourished. The universality of the Gospel is thus forfeited and its inherent claim upon the whole of life. Let us make sure that the candle which we have received is set on the candlestick where

it will give light to *all* in the house; and that the talent
entrusted to us is not diverted from its proper circula-
tion and productivity by being wrapped safely in a
napkin, even in a napkin of the most hallowed and
cherished uses and associations.

INDEX

References in italics indicate citation

Alfred, William, *62 f.*

Berdyaev, N., 19 n.
Bornkamm, G., 117 n.
Brown, John, 85
Buess, Eduard, 47 n.
Bultmann, R., 17, 56, *89, 90 n.*, 98 f.

Campenhausen, Hans von, *75–77*
Copeland, Aaron, *26, 30*
Cullmann, O., 105 f.

Dibelius, M., *39, 86*
Dodd, C. H., 16, 52 n., 53, *86 f., 108 f.*
Duggan, Eileen, *71*

Eliot, T. S., 31

Fridrichsen, A., *57 f.*, 108 n.

Fries, Willy, *91–93*
Frost, Robert, *85*

Goethals, Martha, *29*
Grant, F. C., *58, 97 n., 99 n., 111 f.*

Haenchen, E., 87 n.

Interpretation, 21 n., 24 n.

Jacob, Günther, 56 n.
Journal of Biblical Literature, 99 n.

Klausner, J., *86 f.*
Kraeling, C. H., *69–70*

Lindeskog, G., 108 n.
Lohmeyer, E., *114, 116 n.*

Marsh, John, *88 n.*

Set in Intertype Bodoni
Format by Thomas Geismar
Manufactured by The Haddon Craftsmen, Inc.
Published by HARPER & BROTHERS, *New York*